LEAD GUITAR

By Harvey Vinson.

Wise Publications
London/New York/Sydney
Exclusively distributed by
Music Sales Limited
78 Newman Street
London W1P 3LA
Music Sales Pty. Limited
27 Clarendon Street Artarmon
2064 Sydney

PHOTOGRAPHS

Book design by Jean Hammons and Tara Collins

© Consolidated Music Publishers, 1972

A Division of Music Sales Corporation
All Rights Reserved

International Standard Book Number: 0-8256-4058-X (U.S.A.) 07119 0211 9 (U.K.)
Library of Congress Catalog Card Number: 79-170120

Distributed throughout the world by Music Sales Corporation:

24 East 22nd Street, New York, NY 10010, U.S.A.
78 Newman Street, London W1P 3LA
27 Clarendon Street, Artarmon, Sydney NSW 2064

Printed and bound in Great Britain by Anchor Brendon Ltd, Tiptree, Essex

Contents

. . . I go for that rock 'n' roll music
Any old way you choose it,
It's got a back beat, you can't lose it,
Any old time you use it;
It's gotta be rock 'n' roll music
If you wanna dance with me.
                    —*Chuck Berry*

Introduction

The most important instrumentalist in a rock band is usually the lead guitarist. Many of the big names on the rock scene (Jimi Hendrix, Eric Clapton, B.B. King) established themselves first by their lead guitar work. Not only does the lead guitarist have the responsibility of creating much of the musical excitement in a rock band, but the other musicians in the band usually look to the lead guitarist for musical direction. Further, he is expected to embellish the musical arrangements through creative lead guitar lines. Indeed, the lead guitarist's job "is to trim the pieces with inventive, lyrical guitar licks and to reinforce the rhythm section by playing chops with and against the bass and drums and organ."*

The basic styles of rock, lead improvisation, modulation, rock theory, and more are all discussed in this book. The complete lead guitar trip is here—the rest is up to you.

Good luck. Peace.
— Harvey Vinson

*Excerpt from "The Professional Sound" by Stefan Grossman in *Professional Rock and Roll*, P. 94. New York: Amsco Music Publishing Company, London: Music Sales Limited

Getting Into It

Rock lead guitar is usually played against a rhythmic background consisting of drums, bass guitar, and rhythm guitar (or organ). The enclosed 33⅓ rpm record provides such a background. Play the first side (band two) on your record player. This is blues—or, more properly, rhythm and blues—and is what you'll be improvising lead solos to for the first portion of this book. Listen to this selection a few times and then read on.

Before playing, tune your *electric* guitar* to the record (side one, band one). This recording gives you the correct pitches for all six strings starting with the highest sounding string (1st string) and continuing to the lowest sounding one (6th string).**

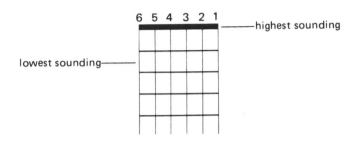

If your guitar is in tune, this G chord should sound quite nice. Place your left hand fingers as close as possible to the indicated frets. The encircled numbers ❶, ❷, ❸, and ❹ represent the index, middle, ring and little fingers, respectively, and are used to indicate the left hand fingering of the various chords and runs. Strum the chord slowly starting with the lowest sounding string. Listen carefully as each string sounds. If any of the strings buzz or sound weak, make sure you have the right fingering and are pressing down hard enough. Fingernails obviously have to go. If the G chord doesn't sound right, try tuning-up again.

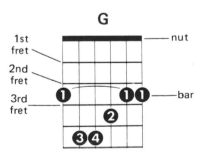

---

*If you're without an electric guitar or guitar amp, see Appendix B for advice on equipment brand names, financial hints, etc. A guitar cable, an adjustable guitar strap, and some guitar picks (flat picks) is the other miscellaneous equipment you need.

**Since there will be times when you won't have your record player with you, detailed tuning instructions are presented later in the book.

Before improvising lead to *any* chord progression, it's a good idea to play through the progression several times with just the chords. This gives you a good "feel" for the chordal structure of the song. With this in mind, learn this next series of chords. Play them in the same manner as you played the G chord.* Make sure all the strings sound clearly.

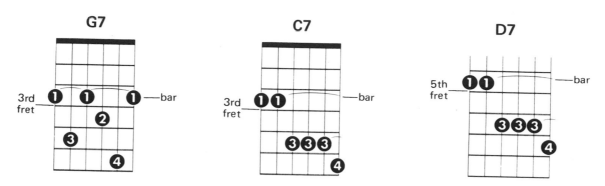

Now count slowly and evenly from 1 to 4 over and over:

Count: 1   2   3   4   1   2   3   4   1   2   3   4   1   2   3   4 etc.

While continuing to count, play the chord indicated above each number using down-strokes of the pick. (In the *down-stroke,* the pick comes into contact with the lowest sounding strings first and moves across the strings toward the ground.) When you come to the end of the progression, start counting and playing immediately from the beginning again.

BLUES IN G #1

Play:	G	G	G	G	G	G	G	G	G	G	G	G	G7	G7	G7	G7
Count:	1	2	3	4	1	2	3	4	1	2	3	4	1	2	3	4

C7	C7	C7	C7	C7	C7	C7	C7	G	G	G	G	G	G	G	G
1	2	3	4	1	2	3	4	1	2	3	4	1	2	3	4

D7	D7	D7	D7	C7	C7	C7	C7	G	G	G	G	D7	D7	D7	D7
1	2	3	4	1	2	3	4	1	2	3	4	1	2	3	4

repeat from
the beginning

*You should be familiar with chords such as these prior to studying this book. If you are you may consider these chord illustrations a review. If not, and they're difficult for you to play, I strongly advise you to first study the book *Rhythm Guitar* published by Consolidated Music Publishers (Music for Millions Series, Volume 57).

After playing this progression a few times on the slow side, speed it up and practice it at a quick tempo. It is an important progression to spend time with.

The chord progression you've been playing is known as the *blues progression* or simply *blues* (also known as the *standard progression*). Originally a chordal vehicle for early Negro sorrow-songs, the blues progression and style attained international recognition in the mid-1910's by such composers as W.C. Handy *(St. Louis Blues).* Not only is this progression the foundation of jazz but, more important, it is the foundation of rock. Every list of top rock tunes always includes songs based on this progression. Rhythm and blues bands (Fats Domino, Chuck Berry) and straight blues bands (Butterfield Blues Band, B.B. King, Albert King) rely mostly on this progression. The technique and style of today's rock scene and the technique and style of rock lead guitar is derived from this progression.

Let's go back to the record. The cut that you've been listening to (side one, band two) is entitled *Blues in G.* This is the same progression you've been working on. Try playing along with the record following the outline of the blues progression on page 7. First, start counting with the record. The second time you count the number "1" begin playing.*

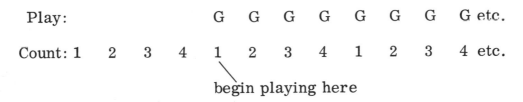

Play: G   G   G   G   G   G   G   G etc.

Count: 1   2   3   4   1   2   3   4   1   2   3   4 etc.

begin playing here

Notice that each chord change is preceded by a short drum roll.

If your playing doesn't sound right to you, practice the exercise on page 7 without the record. Make sure you are:

1)   playing the right chords,
2)   playing with your guitar in tune,
3)   not speeding up (don't play faster than the record).

If your playing reasonably matches the record's, go on to the next chapter.

*Counting before you start playing cues the band to the tempo of the song. On commercial recordings, the counting is generally spliced off the tape (The Young Rascals' *Good Lovin'*—Atlantic 8123-S—is an exception).

Fundamentals

Now that you know how the blues progression sounds, let's learn how it is notated. Lead and rhythm parts are often written on the standard guitar tablature staff:

Vertical lines (called bar lines) divide the staff into measures:

measures

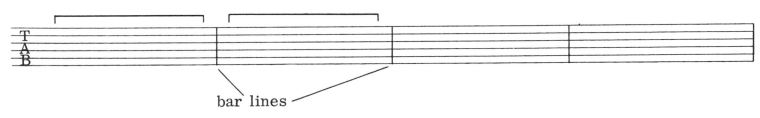

bar lines

A measure is a unit of time consisting of four beats (or counts).

four beats per measure

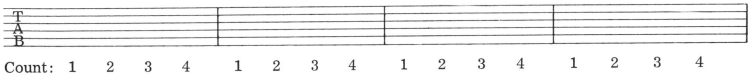

Count: 1   2   3   4   1   2   3   4   1   2   3   4   1   2   3   4

Wedge-marks (///) on the staff indicate that you strum a chord. The letter name of the chord is located above the wedge-mark.

chord symbol (the chord to strum)

G   wedge-mark (means that you strum)

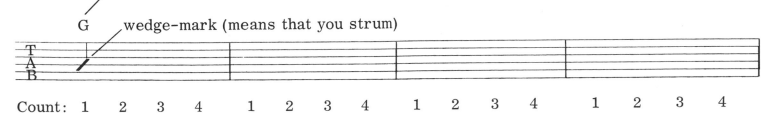

Count: 1   2   3   4   1   2   3   4   1   2   3   4   1   2   3   4

When you strum a chord once on each count (as in the first chapter) four wedge-marks appear in each measure. Count and play this short example.

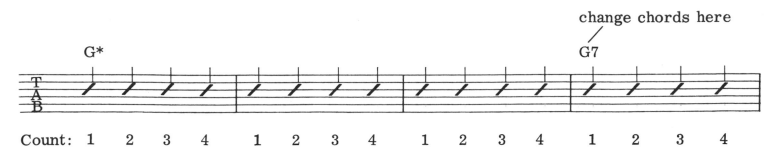

change chords here

Using this system, here is the entire *Blues in G* from the first chapter. Notice how much easier it is to read.

BLUES IN G #2

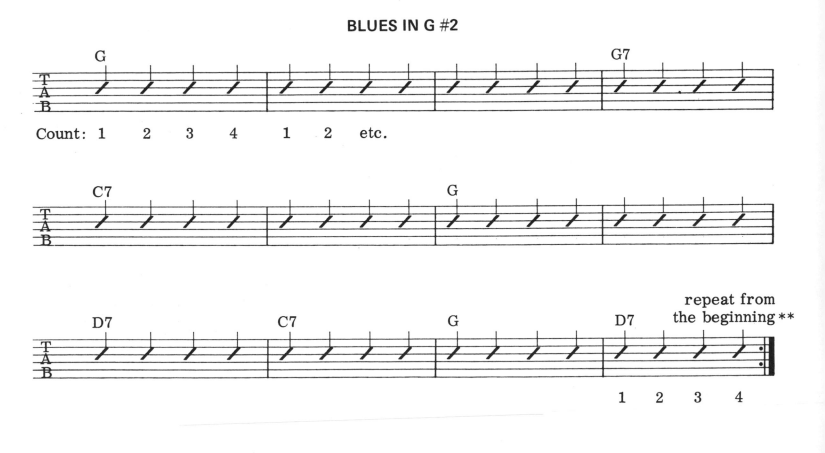

Play the progression through a few times using this outline (with or without the record). Keep your eyes on the page, not on your left hand. Compare it to the previous blues outline.

Count the number of measures in *Blues in G;* you'll find it to be 12 measures (or bars) long. If you repeat the progression, the length is 12 times two. Although the length of the blues progression varied originally from 8 to 16 bars, it has become fixed by today's rock players at 12 bars. It is referred to as "12 bar blues" no matter how many repeats you take.

*Once a chord is indicated, use that chord until a new one is called for. In this case, play the G chord for the first three measures then the G7 chord in the 4th measure.

**Continue to the first measure and play the G chord on the next "1" count.

Riffs

Let's learn a lead guitar solo! First, examine the tablature staff again. Each of the six lines represents a guitar string: the top line stands for the highest sounding string, the next line stands for the next string down, and so forth. The bottom line stands for the lowest sounding string.

TABLATURE   GUITAR STRINGS

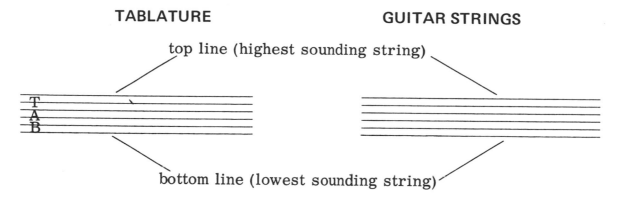

top line (highest sounding string)

bottom line (lowest sounding string)

Arabic numbers on the tablature staff indicate the specific string and fret positions to play. A "3" on the bottom line indicates that you play the lowest sounding string fretted at the 3rd fret. Left hand fingering appears immediately below the tab note. Thus:

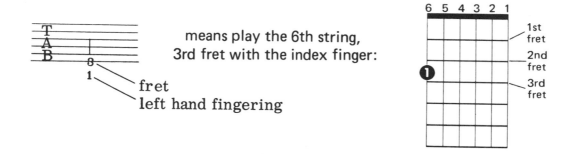

means play the 6th string, 3rd fret with the index finger:

fret
left hand fingering

While fingering the above note, the left hand looks like this:

Note that the string is depressed immediately behind the 3rd fret by the tip of the 1st finger. Also note the position of the thumb.

A "5" on the next line up indicates that you play the 5th string fretted at the 5th fret.

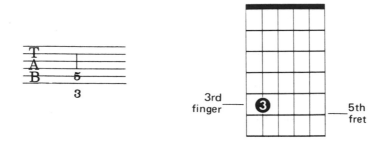

A "3" on the fourth line from the top has you playing the 4th string fretted at the 3rd fret.

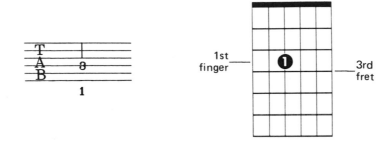

A "5" on the fourth line from the top employs the 4th string fretted at the 5th fret.

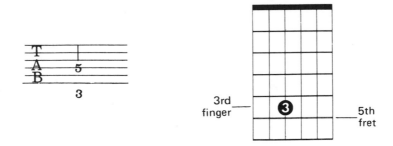

These four notes can be combined to play a lead guitar riff.* Count from 1 to 4 playing one note on each beat. Use only down-strokes of the pick.

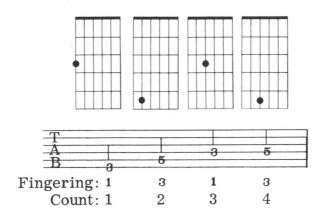

Play it through a few times until you can play it with ease.

In preparation for *Blues in G* solo, move the entire riff over one string, and play it a few times (the first note of the riff is now on the 5th string). Keep the same left hand fingering.

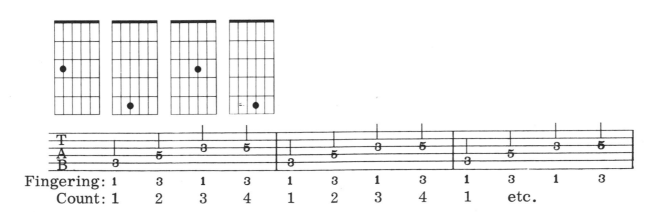

*A *riff* is a short, melodic phrase which is usually repeated.

Keeping the first note of the riff on the 5th string, move the riff up two frets (towards you) and play it a few times. After learning the riff in this position you'll be able to play the first lead solo.

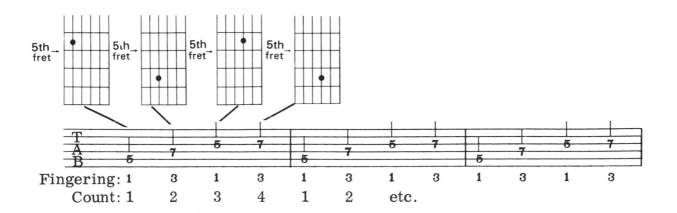

Now for the solo. Look it over before you start playing. Notice that the riff changes position at each chord change (A G chord to a G7 chord is not a chord change). Practice the solo a few times and then try it with the rhythm background of the *Blues in G* (side one). The chord symbols above the tab staff tell you where you are in relation to the blues progression.

BLUES IN G #3

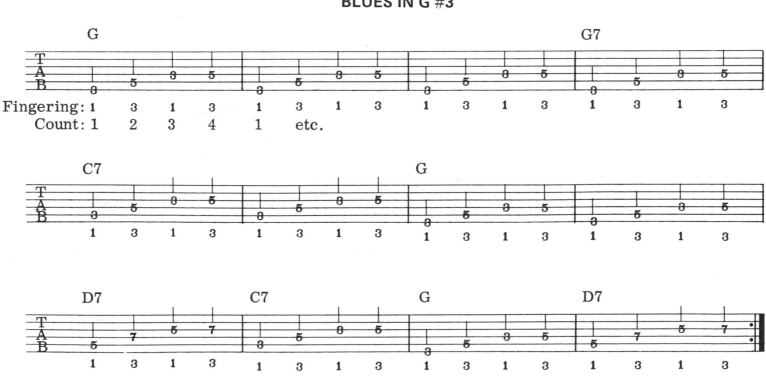

The repetition of a melodic riff in the blues progression runs throughout the history of rock. Even in the 1920's, a full 30 years before rock, barrelhouse pianists were pounding out 12 bar boogie-woogie with its repetitive left hand (bass note) patterns. The chordal structure of the blues lends itself to this concept. Used from the early days of rock (Bill Doggett's *Honky Tonk* *) to the late 60's (the Cream's *Sunshine Of Your Love*), the riff repetition in the blues progression has become a standard rock idiom.

*Doggett's guitarist, Billy Butler, plays some very instructive lead work on the album containing this song (*The Best Of Bill Doggett,* King 908).

More Riffs

Once you start playing lead riffs, dozens of riff ideas will start popping into your head. Riff lead playing follows an easily understandable formula which partially accounts for the popularity of this style of playing. It only takes one four note riff to get you through the entire blues progression! First, take a one measure riff* that can be played against a G chord:

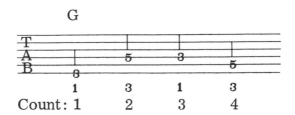

Play this one measure riff whenever a G (or G7) chord appears in the blues progression.

BLUES IN G #4

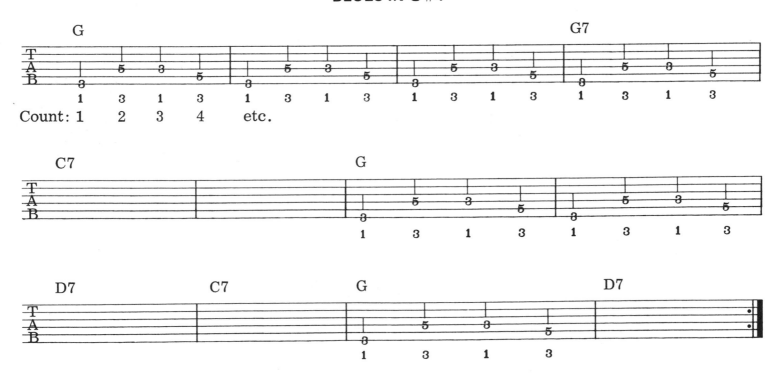

Play the same riff with the same fingering starting on the 5th string everytime a C7 chord appears.

*This riff is a slight variation of the first one you learned.

BLUES IN G #4

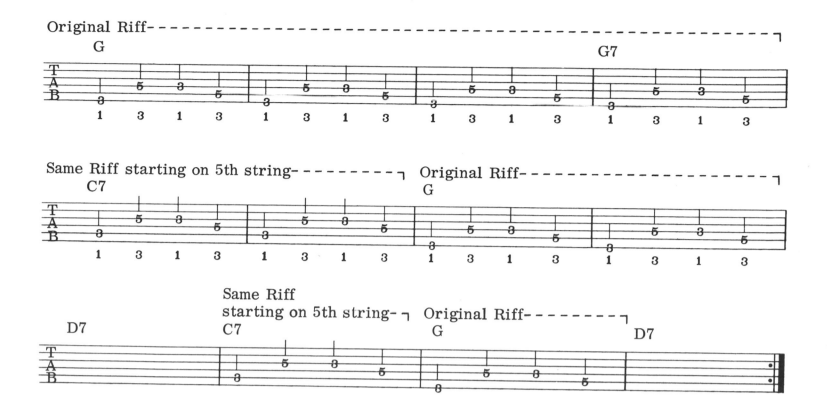

With the riff starting on the 5th string, raise it two frets. Play the riff in this position everytime a D7 chord appears in the blues progression. Make sure you understand this formula before going on.

BLUES IN G #4

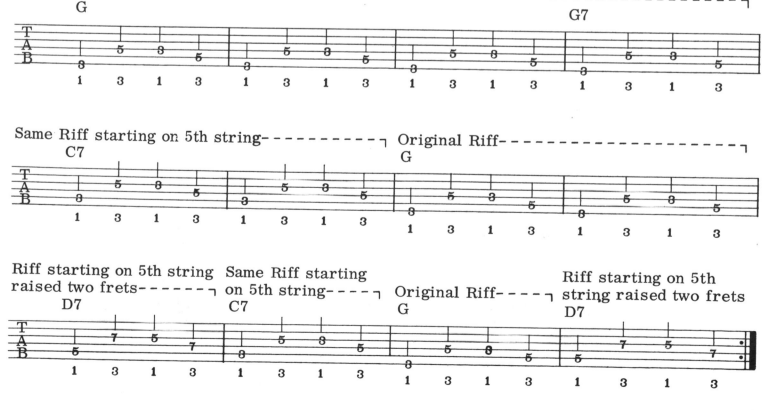

So now you have another lead solo to play with the record. Compare this one to the solo in the previous chapter.

To create a new solo, all you need is a different one measure riff. Once you have a new riff, use the formula presented in this chapter to construct the solo. Play this next riff a few times. The first note is repeated so take care.

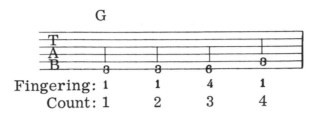

Now play a solo using this riff. For variety, play the blues solo from the previous chapter for the first chorus (first time through the blues progression), the second lead solo for the second chorus, and the last solo for the third chorus.

For a new solo learn this riff. The left hand fingering is a little different than in the others.

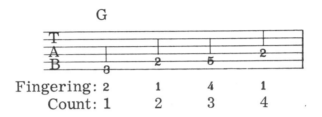

I could give you a mini-dictionary of riffs to memorize but a much better idea is to make up some of your own. For now the only requirement is that the first riff should sound good played against a G chord. Play the G chord a few times to get the sound of it in your ear and then compose your own riff. You'll have an easier time of it if you'll make this the first note:

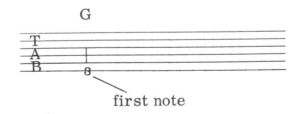

After you've created a good riff, the rest is easy.

Rhythm and Things

Up to now, you've been playing one note on each beat. Because of its time value this note is a quarter note and is identified by a single stem.

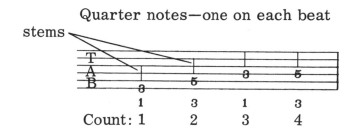

Quarter notes—one on each beat

stems

Count: 1 2 3 4

Another important time value is the eighth note. Eighth notes are played two on each beat and are connected by a beam. Count "and" between each beat when playing this new rhythm.

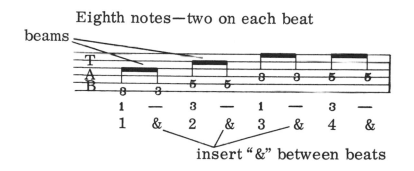

Eighth notes—two on each beat

beams

insert "&" between beats

Pick direction is important when you play eighth notes. On the beat use a down-stroke ⊓ moving the pick away from you towards the ground. On the "&" between the beats use an up-stroke ∨ moving the pick towards you. Here's the last riff with pick directions.

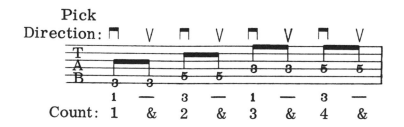

Pick
Direction: ⊓ ∨ ⊓ ∨ ⊓ ∨ ⊓ ∨

Count: 1 & 2 & 3 & 4 &

And, of course, a one measure eighth note riff functions in the lead formula the same way as a one measure quarter note riff. Play the next solo to better understand this. It uses a slight (but improved) variation of the last eighth note riff. Pay particular attention to the pick directions.

BLUES IN G #5

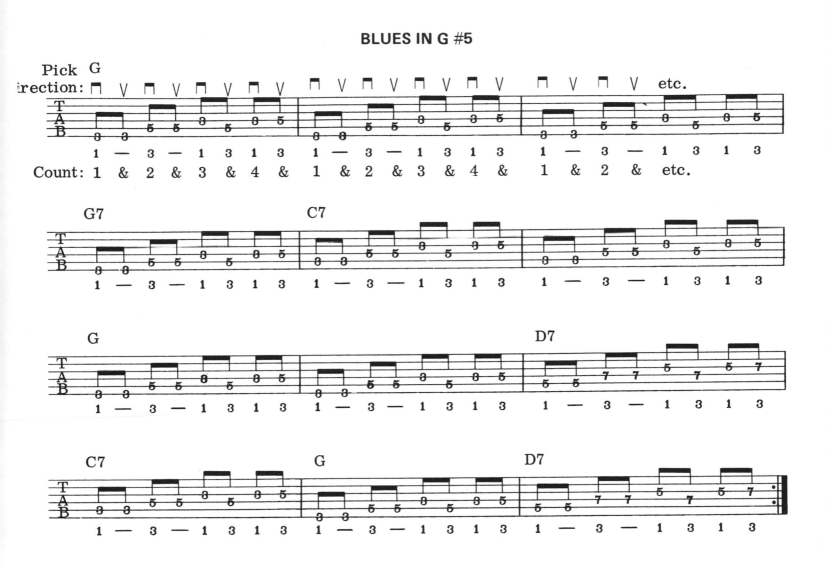

Learn this next eighth note riff for a new lead solo. It's an exciting one so practice it well.

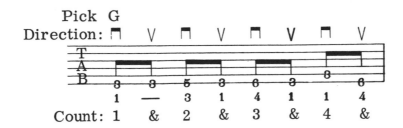

After you have it in your fingers, use it with the lead formula for a new solo.

Quarter notes and eighth notes are often used together in the same one measure riff. In this next riff, play eighth notes on the 2nd and 4th beats and quarter notes on the 1st and 3rd beats.

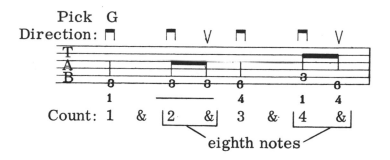

Using the last riff you can play still another lead solo with the record!

An important device that improves the rhythm of a riff is the tie: ⌣ . When two notes of the same pitch are tied together, sustain the sound of the first note through the time value of the second note. Suppose you had this to play:

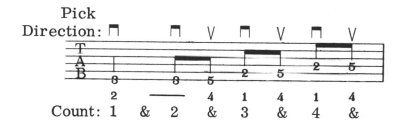

Here's the same riff with the first and second notes tied together. Sustain the sound of the first note, do not play the second note. The next note you would play is on the "&" after the "2." Try it.

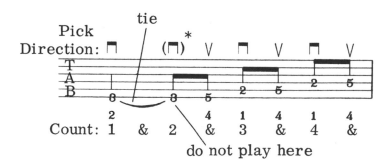

*Although you don't play this note, move the pick down in order to prepare for the up-stroke.

Play this lead solo using the last riff.

BLUES IN G #6

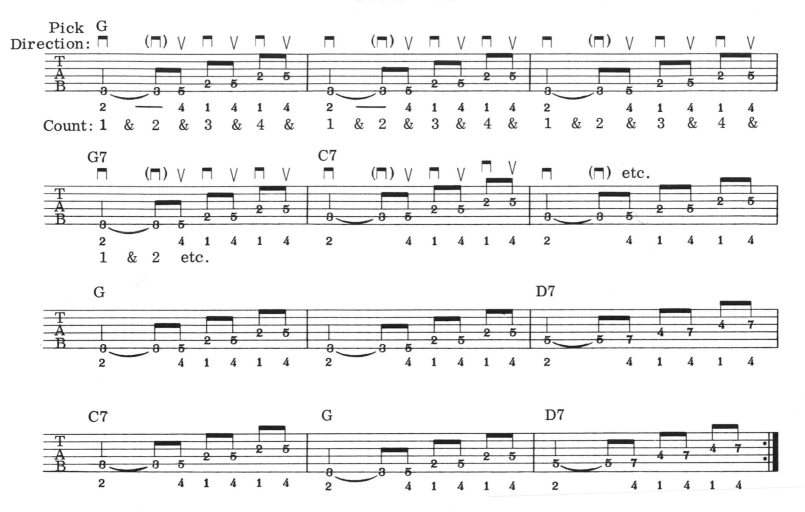

This next riff makes use of two ties. The notes on both the "2" and the "4" beats are tied to the previous notes. Practice quite slowly making sure you're playing the right time values.

Play a lead solo using this riff.

Longer Riffs

One of the important techniques used in lead improvisation is the concept of question and answer. This can be done by extending the length of the riff from one measure to two measures. Play this two measure riff:

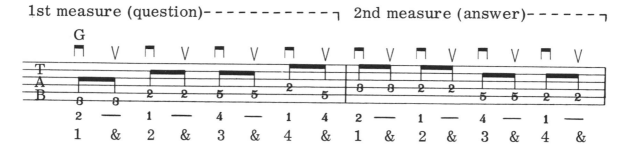

The first measure is answered by the second measure. Clearly, these two measures compliment each other and make a unified musical statement.

A two measure riff works similarly to the one measure riff in the blues progression. Play the two measure riff whenever a G chord appears in the blues progression. When the progression calls for only one measure of G (measure 11), play only the first measure of the riff.

BLUES IN G #7

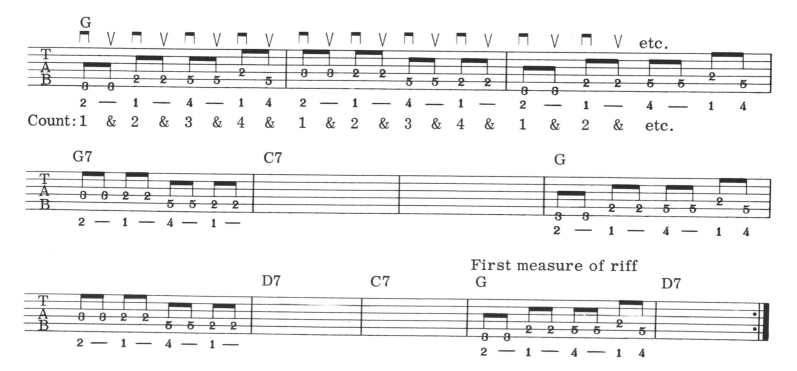

Whenever a C7 chord appears, play the same two measure riff starting on the 5th string. When the blues progression calls for only one measure of C7, as in measure 10, play the first measure of the riff. For the D7 chord use only the first measure of the riff (raised two frets, starting on the 5th string). After you're familiar with the construction of the solo, play it with the record.

BLUES IN G #7

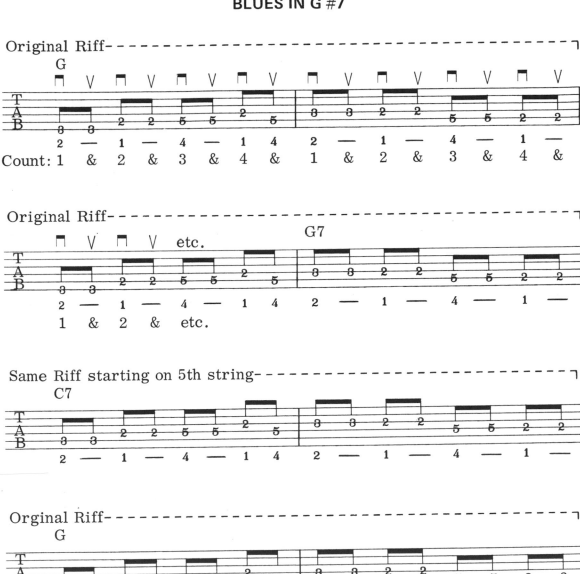

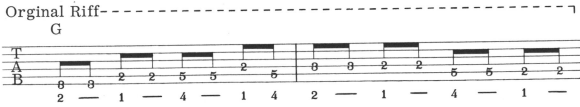

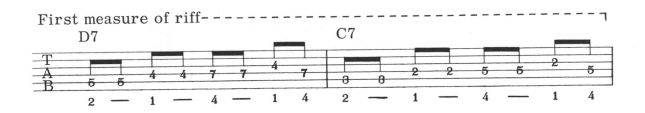

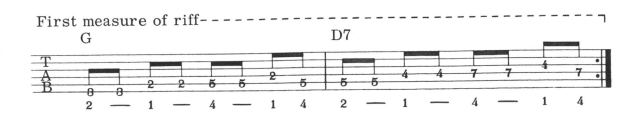

Here's another two measure riff. This one makes use of the tie. Practice it quite slowly at first making sure not to play on the "2" of the second measure.

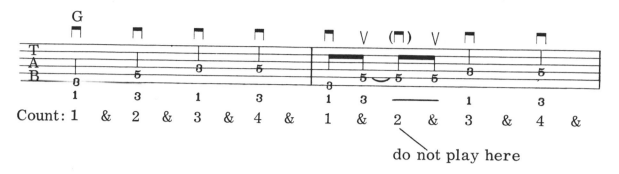

do not play here

After you've learned the last riff, play another solo using the two measure riff technique. Be sure to play only the first measure of the riff in the last four measures of the progression.

Try this more sophisticated two measure riff for a new blues lead:

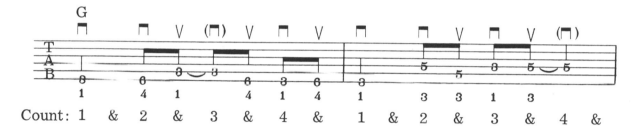

Remember—play only the first measure of the riff in the last four measures of the progression.

Try making up 2nd measures of your own and tagging them on to some of your favorite one measure riffs presented earlier. Keep in mind that the 2nd measure of the riff should "answer" and compliment the 1st measure.

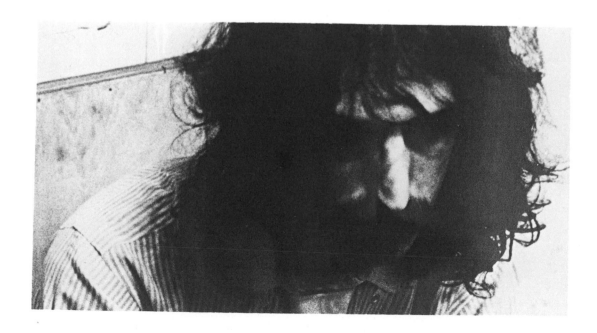

Heavier Riffs

A popular lead technique is to begin the riff slightly before the measure. This anticipates the riff and gives it more forward motion. In the next example, the first note of the riff is played on the "&" before the "1." Pay particular attention to pick directions.

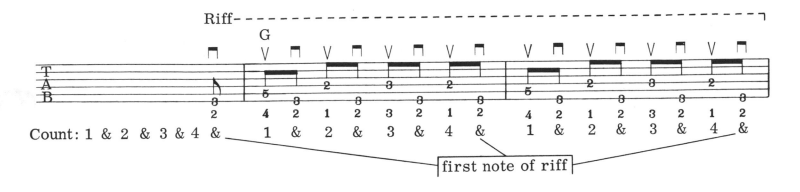

first note of riff

The difference in playing this type of riff and the regular one is that you'll have to change your left hand position a half beat earlier when the chords change.

BLUES IN G #8

Count: 4 & 1 & 2 & 3 & 4 & 1 & 2 & 3 & 4 & 1 & 2 & 3 & 4 &

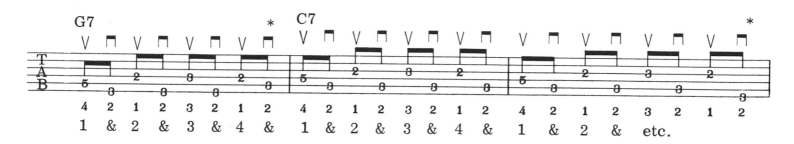

1 & 2 & 3 & 4 & 1 & 2 & 3 & 4 & 1 & 2 & etc.

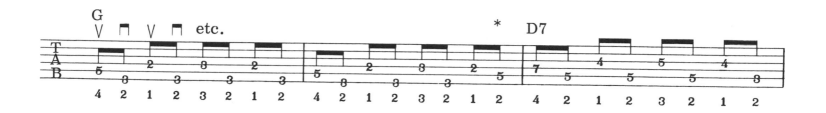

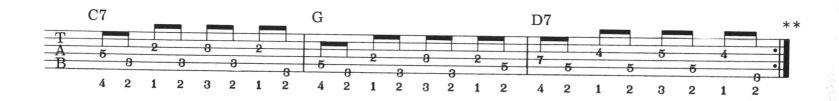

Here's a riff for another lead solo. This one begins three notes before the measure (on the "&" after "3"). There are some new notes so practice carefully.

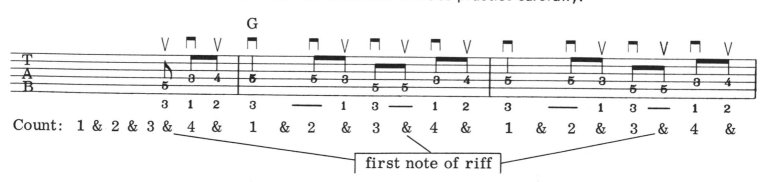

Count: 1 & 2 & 3 & 4 & 1 & 2 & 3 & 4 & 1 & 2 & 3 & 4 &

first note of riff

*Change left hand position here

**Repeat everything between these two signs:

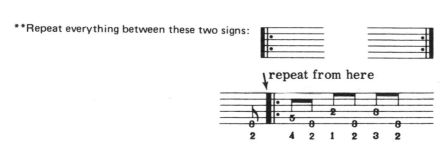

repeat from here

Since the riff begins on the "&" after "3," the left hand changes positions at this point before the chords change. One other thing—the last measure of the blues progression (12th measure) frequently breaks the usual sequence to add interest as the progression returns to the first measure. The solo illustrates this technique.

BLUES IN G #9

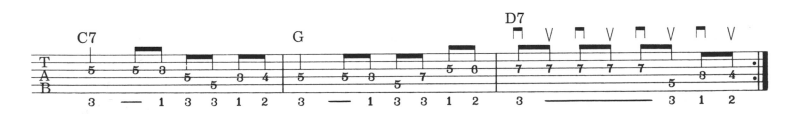

Another popular lead riff is achieved by playing two strings with one stroke of the pick. In the next example play the 5th and 6th strings together with each pick stroke. When two or more strings are played at one time, the left hand fingerings are stacked under the tab notes. The top number is the fingering for the highest note, the number below is the fingering for the next note, etc. You'll have to stretch your left hand fingers a bit to play this one.

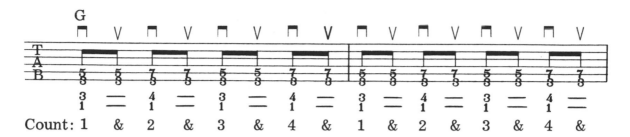

A new solo to play! Another popular 12th bar riff is used in the last measure of the progression. This rift could be used in the last measure of any of the solos you've studied up to now.

BLUES IN G #10

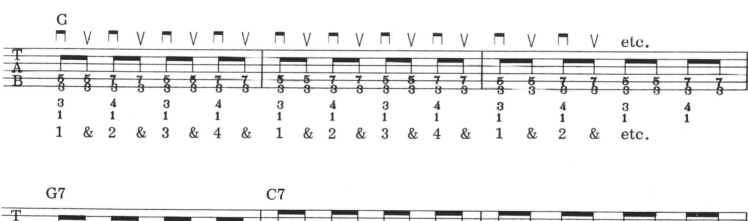

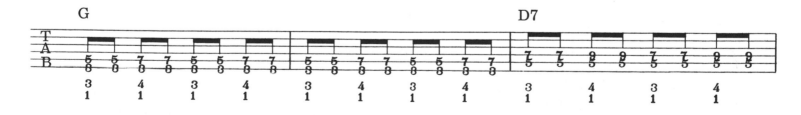

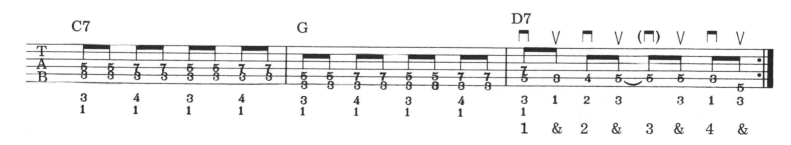

Some riffs have more drive when played using the staccato effect. The idea of the staccato effect is to make the sound of the note stop an instant after it is sounded (*staccato* is an Italian word meaning "detached"). It's really quite easy. First play this note.

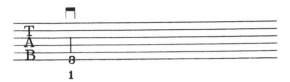

As soon as the note sounds, relax the fretting left hand finger. This stops the sound of the string. Take care, however, to leave the left hand finger in contact with the string. Don't lift the finger up, just relax it. A dot over the note indicates this technique.

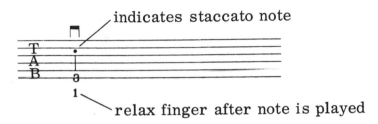

The last solo sounds quite nice played staccato. Relax both left hand fretting fingers each time you strum. Try this example:

Now go back and play the solo again using this new technique. Play every measure staccato except the 12th measure.

THE OTIS REDDING DICTIONARY OF SOUL COMPLETE & UNBELIEVABLE

Ou - yea (ū′ yā′) adv. — to give in; a reply to get what one wants.

My - my - my (mī) poss. adj. — no longer yours; goody three times.

Ou - ni (ū′ nī′) adv. — to hurt so good.

Ni (nī) adv. — to do very quickly.

Leetle (lēt′ l) adj. — just enough to make one want more.

Ou (ū) n. — ouchless excitement.

Yea - ni (yā′ nī) adv. — an agreement to give in very quickly.

Oh - mi (ō′ mī) interj + adv (comp) — to get it very quickly.

Weel (wēl) n., v., aux. v., v. t. — desire to give it or get it.

Gotta - Gotta (gŏt′ tă) v. — not able to do without it.

Give it (gĭv′ ĭt) v + pron (comp) — absitively posilutely not.

Oh - naw - naw (ō nă′) interj + adv (comp) — to let oneself go, under any circumstances.

Fa - fa - fa - fa - fa (fă) phrase — sad song.

Ou we ni (ū′ wē nī) phrase — getting gooder by the minute.

Reprinted From *The Otis Redding Dictionary of Soul,* Volt 415, by Permission of Paramount Music Publishing Companies (East/Memphis Music BMI)

Country Blues

The first musicians to popularize the guitar as a serious blues instrument were country blues guitarists. Before any electrified R & B bands of the 30's and 40's existed, country blues guitarists were laying the foundation of the blues and rock movement. The advent of race records in the 20's brought limited attention to these artists. Later, record companies such as Columbia sent roving talent scouts deep into the South to record them. Many of their techniques are used by present-day lead guitarists—country blues riffs being among the more popular of them.

This style of riffing is derived from standard chord formations. First, re-acquaint yourself with the G blues chords.

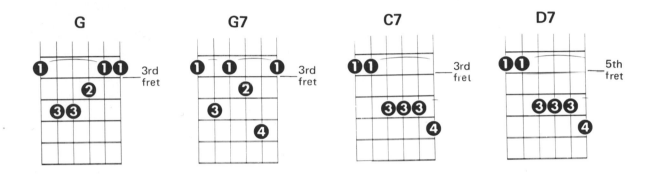

This next riff is a banjo strum adapted for guitar. It is not surprising that banjo riffs found their way to the guitar as the banjo (or *banjar*) was an African instrument and was played by many wandering Negro minstrels in the late 19th century. The riff uses only the top three strings of the guitar. Finger the entire G chord and then play the riff—watch the pick directions as they are tricky.*

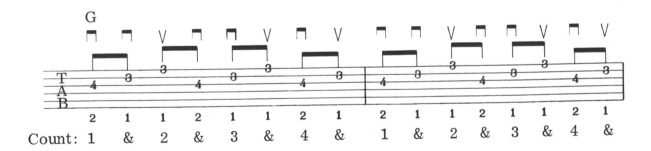

*Many guitarists consider the pick technique the hardest part of the riff. The riff is easier to play using your right hand fingers to pluck the strings: thumb playing the 3rd string, index finger playing the 2nd string, middle finger playing the 1st string. Using only the least demanding techniques, however, is a short cut to mediocrity.

When playing this type of riff, most guitarists finger only the top three or four strings of the chord being played. This makes it easier for the left hand. Try these:

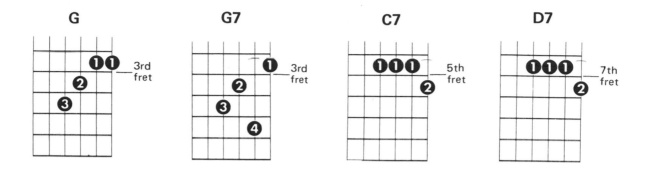

Use these fingerings for the first country blues solo. When you come to a chord change in the progression, finger all four strings at the same time.

COUNTRY BLUES #1

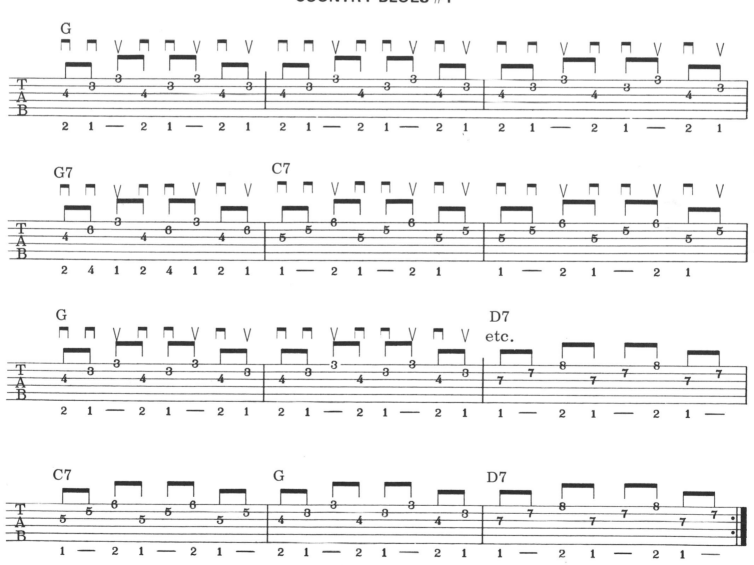

Another popular country blues riff:

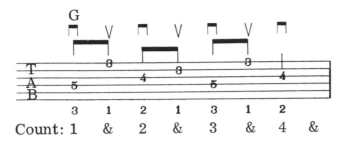

When playing this riff, finger only the top four strings of the chord. Here's the same riff as played on the C7 and D7 chords:

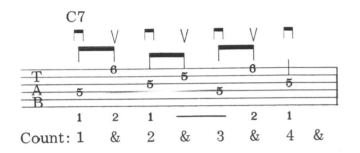

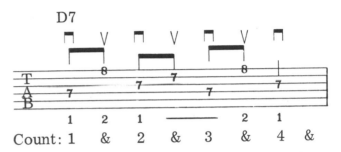

Play a new solo using the last riff.

Combining the two, you have a beautiful two bar riff. Try this:

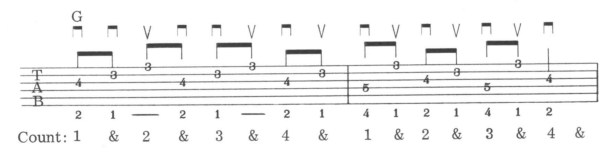

Play a lead with this two measure riff using the appropriate formula.

Once you get the feel for this type of riff, you'll be able to make up some of your own. Here's another popular two bar riff to play as a solo. (Again, use the two measure riff formula.)

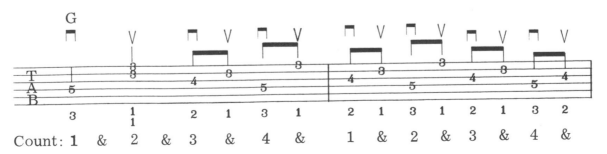

Notes Produced By 6th String

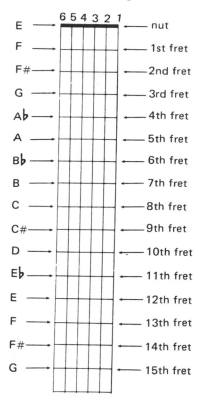

	6 5 4 3 2 1	
E →		nut
F →		← 1st fret
F# →		← 2nd fret
G →		← 3rd fret
Ab →		← 4th fret
A →		← 5th fret
Bb →		← 6th fret
B →		← 7th fret
C →		← 8th fret
C# →		← 9th fret
D →		← 10th fret
Eb →		← 11th fret
E →		← 12th fret
F →		← 13th fret
F# →		← 14th fret
G →		← 15th fret

Another popular country blues riff technique is the use throughout the progression of the same chord formation. The most practical chord formation for this technique is the *root 6 bar chord.* To understand how and where to locate this chord formation, it's necessary to know the notes produced by the 6th string. Examine the illustrated note chart. Included in the chart are the notes the 6th string produces at each fret. When you fret behind the 3rd fret the 6th string produces the note G; behind the 5th fret the 6th string produces the note A; behind the 8th fret C; behind the 10th fret D; etc. Try going up and down the 6th string a few times playing and naming the notes out loud.

Both the G and the G7 chords you've been playing are *root 6 bar chords,* whose letter name is determined by the position the bar takes on the 6th string. When you finger either the G or the G7 chord, locate the bar behind the 3rd fret.

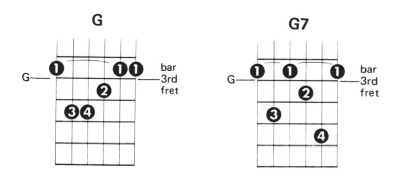

By locating the G7 chord formation behind the 8th fret, you have a C7 chord:

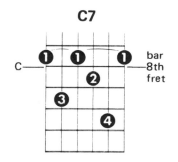

Behind the 10th fret, a D7 chord:

D7

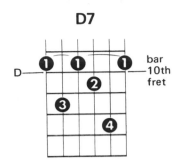

It's easy to see that the G7 chord formation behind any one of the 15 frets indicated in the note chart would produce a different 7th chord. First locate the letter name of the desired chord on the 6th string, and then make the 7th chord formation behind that fret. Follow the same procedure for locating major chords using the G chord formation. Try playing through the *G Blues* with only *root 6 bar chords* in preparation for the next solo.

Using the first riff in this lesson with only *root 6 bar chords* creates a new solo with an old riff. When a chord change is called for, simply move the entire chord formation to the new fret. As before, finger only the top four strings of the chord.

COUNTRY BLUES #2

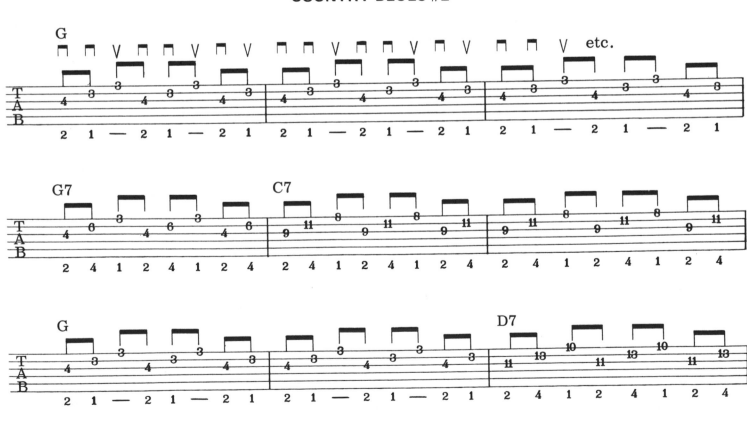

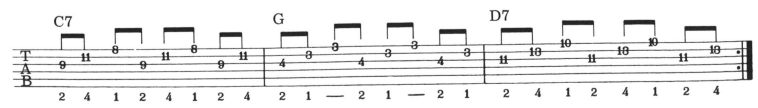

Other more melodic country blues riffs can be played with *root 6 bar chords*. Try this next example. Finger the top three strings of the G chord throughout the entire measure.

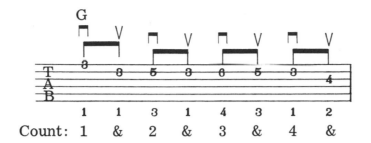

With melodic riffs, change chords by merely moving the riff (bar and all) to the new fret. To play the riff with the C7 chord, move the entire riff to the 8th fret and play it. For the D7 chord, move the riff to the 10th fret. To the solo!

COUNTRY BLUES #3

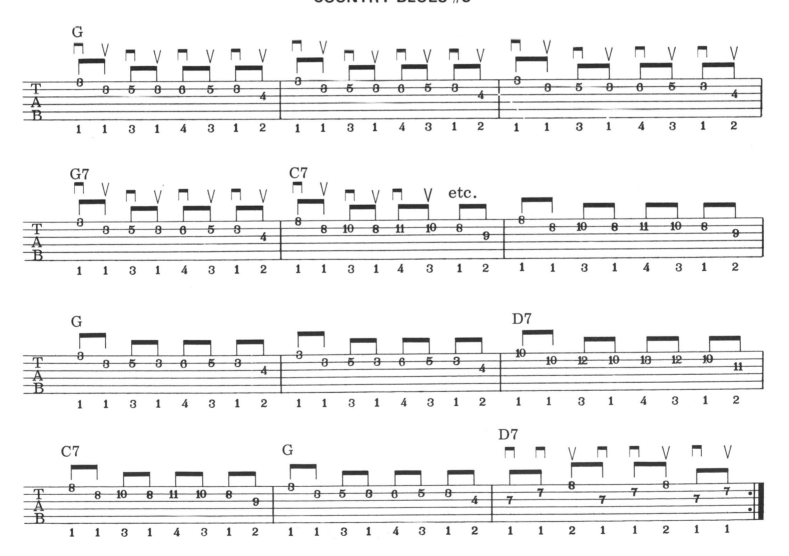

Examine the next melodic country riff. Notice that several of the notes are tied together. When two notes *of different pitches* are tied together, play only the first note with the pick. While the string is still ringing, hammer-down the indicated left hand finger to make the second note sound. Don't play the second note with the pick—the left hand alone produces the sound.

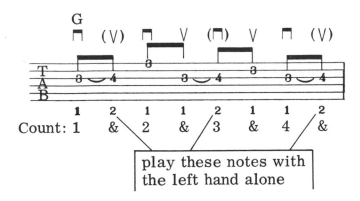

This is difficult to play well so spend some time with it. After you can play it, take a solo using only *root 6 bar chords.*

To top off this chapter, here's a Chuck Berry style solo. The last four bars of the solo make use of two different country blues riffs. Mixing riffs of the same flavor adds interest to any solo.

BLUES IN G #11

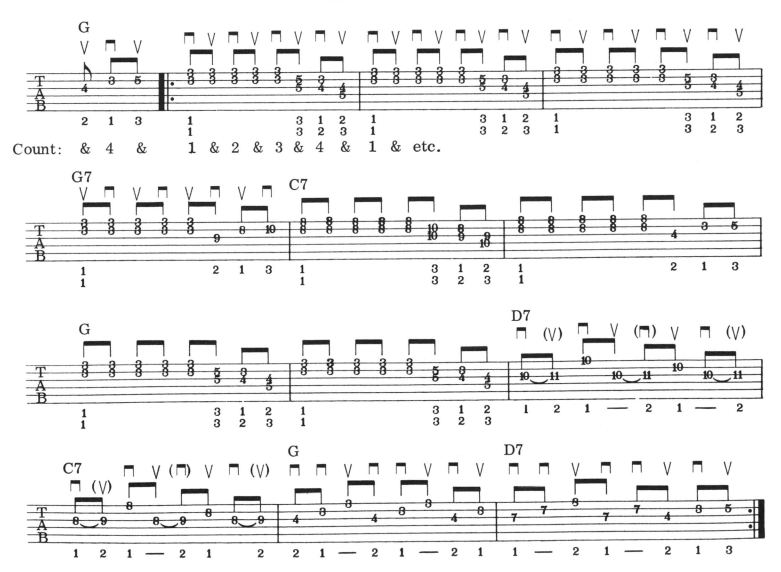

Turn On, Tune Up

Since there will be times when you won't have your tuning record (or record player) you must learn other ways to tune your guitar. When you're playing along and something just doesn't sound right, you can almost bet that your guitar is out of tune. The more you play with a tuned guitar, the easier you can tell when it is out of tune. The person who suffers the most from an out-of-tune instrument is you and your ears. So keep your instrument in tune!

When you're playing in a group, tune your guitar to the other instruments in the band. If there is an organ or an electric piano in the band, tune to that since its pitch is fixed. Otherwise, choose the instrument that is closest to being perfectly in tune and use that as your standard.

When tuning to an organ (or a piano), the 1st string on the guitar (high E) corresponds to the E above middle C. The 6th string (low E) produces a sound two octaves below that. Here is a diagram which shows you how to find the notes you'll need.

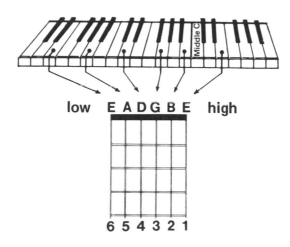

Another method to get your guitar in tune uses a guitar pitch pipe. When in tune, each string on the guitar produces a specific note that corresponds to one of the notes of the pitch pipe.

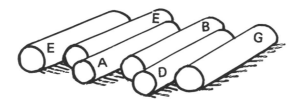

The most widely used (and best) method of tuning is unfortunately the most difficult. Start by assuming that the 6th string (low E) is fairly on pitch.* If it seems too high (tight), loosen the string a bit; if it seems too low (loose and buzzing), turn the peg to tighten the string a little.

*If a harmonica is available, use it to tune this string. Blowing out on the 1 hole of an E harp produces E—sucking in on the 1 hole of a D harp also produces E.

When the 6th string sounds all right to you, fret it at the 5th fret. At the same time, pluck the string—the note you get will be an A, the correct note for the open A (5th) string. Tune the 5th string.

same sound as

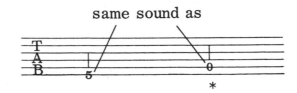

*

When the 5th string is in tune with the 6th string, fret it at the 5th fret. This will give you the correct note to tune the open D (4th) string to.

same sound as

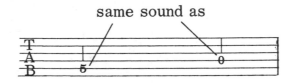

When that string is in tune, fret it (the 4th string) at the 5th fret. This gives you a G. Tune the open 3rd string.

same sound as

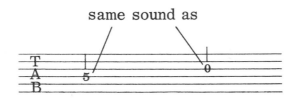

Now fret the 3rd string at the 4th fret. This gives you the correct note to tune the open B (2nd) string.

same sound as

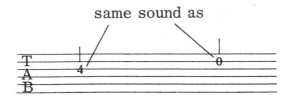

Finally, fret the 2nd string at the 5th fret to tune the open 1st string.

same sound as

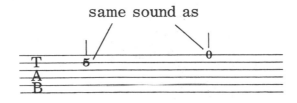

*An ''o'' indicates an open or unfingered string.

40

When you've done all that, strum some of the chords you know to check your tuning. You might have to go over your tuning a few times until you get the right sounds. Happiness is a tuned guitar!

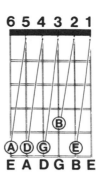

The Blues Scale

When a band performs a song, they generally play it in a set *form.* The form of a song is the organization of the piece as a succession of sections. One of the more frequently used forms is the singing of two or three verses of the song followed by an instrumental (lead) break concluding the song with a final verse. Everytime the song is played, the band uses the same form, the same basic rhythms, and usually the same bass lines. The greatest deviation is the lead guitar work—particularly in the improvised instrumental breaks. Improvisation is the spontaneous creation and development of musical ideas, and this improvisation is the main task of the lead guitarist. Here is the musician who must coax creative energy from his instrument making the songs (and the band) more exciting and interesting. The better the lead guitarist, the more meaningful the songs.

Most of the notes that lead guitarists use in their improvisations are derived from an important rock scale known as the blues scale. The blues scale in the key of G is fingered and played as follows. Try it:

BLUES SCALE

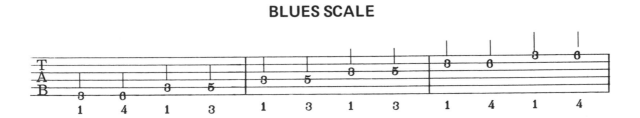

A fingerboard diagram of the blues scale looks like this:

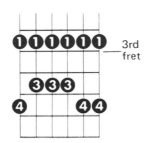

Beginning with the first finger on the 3rd fret of the 6th string, every other note in the blues scale is fingered by the 1st finger of the left hand.

This next exercise takes you up and down the blues scale. Play it perfectly as it is extremely important to master this scale.

42

EXERCISE #1

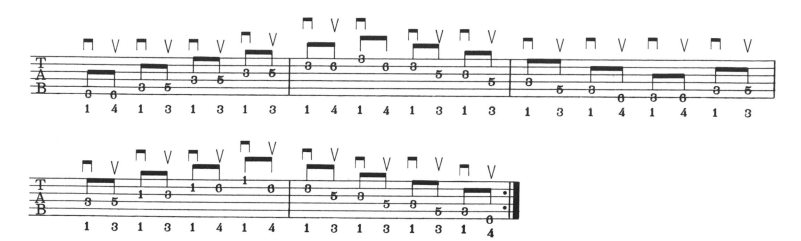

Once you get the blues scale solidly in your fingers, a new world will begin to unfold. You'll be able to create and play entire solos based on your own technical skill and musical knowledge! When improvising, however, it is essential to confine your playing to the notes of the blues scale. But enough of this—let's get back to the actual playing. This next solo will give you a better feel for the scale. The solo is constructed from the blues scale and uses the two bar riff pattern as its foundation.

BLUES IN G #12

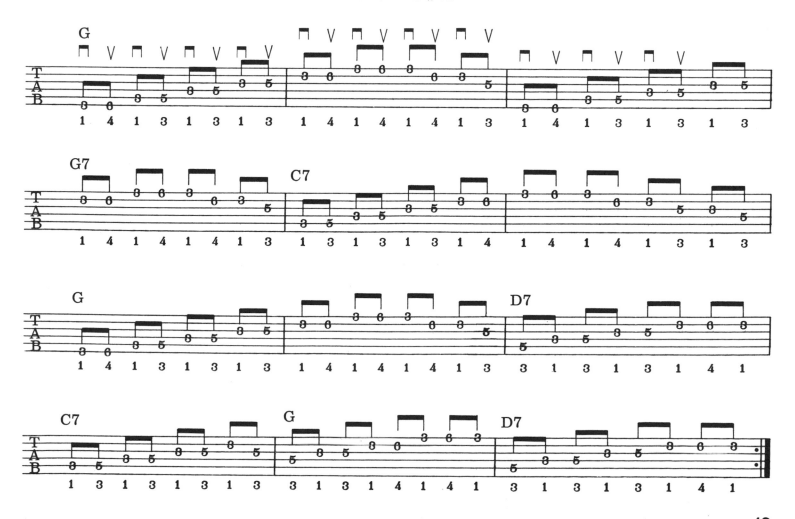

The hammer-down technique sounds quite nice used in the blues scale. The opposite of this technique is the *snap-off.* When two notes of different pitches are tied together and the *first* note is higher in pitch, play only the first note with the pick. While the string is still ringing, snap-off the fretting left hand finger making the second note sound. Don't play the second note with the pick—the left hand alone produces the sound. With the snap-off, the lower note must be fretted when you play the upper note.

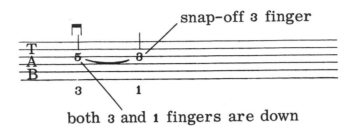

Here's the last solo using both the hammer-down and the snap-off techniques. When you finger the 3rd string with the 1st finger going up the scale, fret the top three strings with a small bar. This prepares the fingering for the top of the scale and allows you to play somewhat faster.

BLUES IN G #13

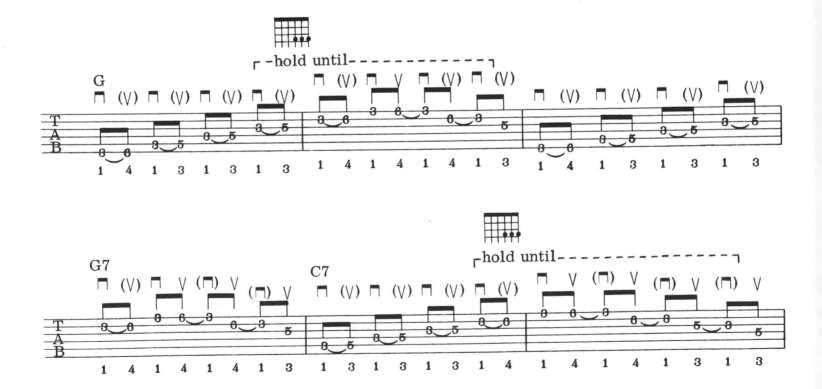

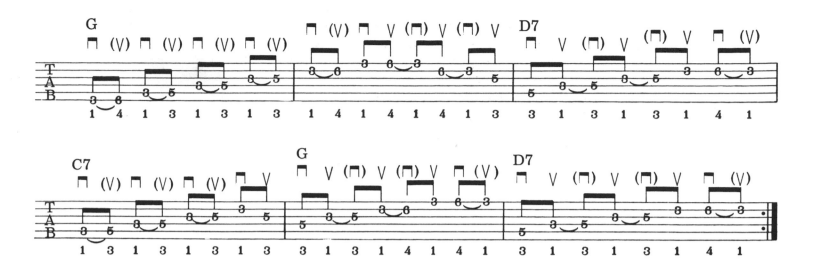

The hammer-down and snap-off techniques are used quite frequently by lead guitarists, so spend some time with this solo. If your left hand starts to sweat and ache as you're playing, stop and relax for awhile. Using light gauge strings will make this solo easier to play. La Bella *Extra Slinky* strings and Guild *Sidewinder* strings are two brand names used by professionals.

Playing the next solo will add to your technique and your knowledge of the blues scale. It starts at the top of the scale and works its way down using both hammer-downs and snap-offs. Again, bar the first three strings with the 1st finger of the left hand when playing the top part of the blues scale.

BLUES IN G #14

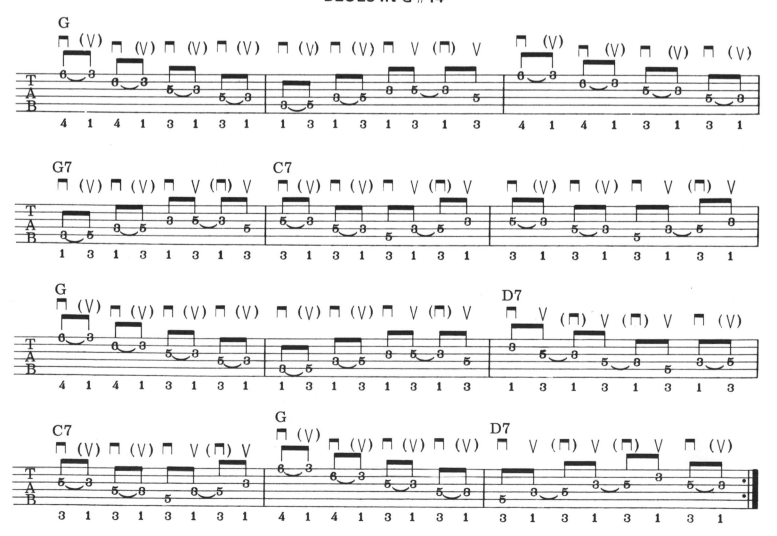

Improvisation

The ability to improvise implies thinking and creating music *while you're playing.* It is not a mystical ability but can be learned. The effectiveness of improvisation is judged on how well the improvised part relates to the song; both to the preceding as well as the succeeding sections. It is used to weld the different parts of the song together.

The style of most rock improvisation is derived from the blues progression—the concept of question and answer. The question and answer formula is divided between the singer and the lead guitarist. The singer sings two bars of the song (question) with the next two bars consisting of an improvised answer by the lead guitarist. The lead guitarist improvises an instrumental answer to the vocalist's question. The origin of this technique is the call and response patterns used in early Negro work songs.

With this style of improvisation, the tie is frequently used across the bar line. When this occurs, do not play on the "1." As an example:

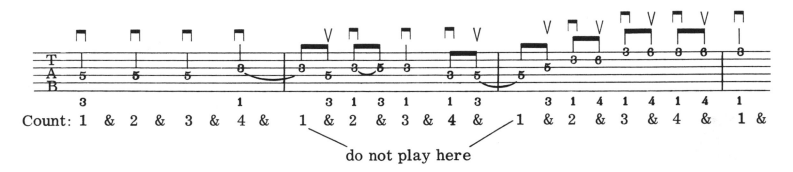

Now for the song. Before playing, examine the song carefully noting the two bar question and answer patterns. Try learning the words first and sing them using the notated melody (or a variation) with the record. After you've done that, sing the melody and play the instrumental answers. This is the way the blues is sung and played. (As Albert King once said, "This is blues power, baby!")

BLUES IN G #15

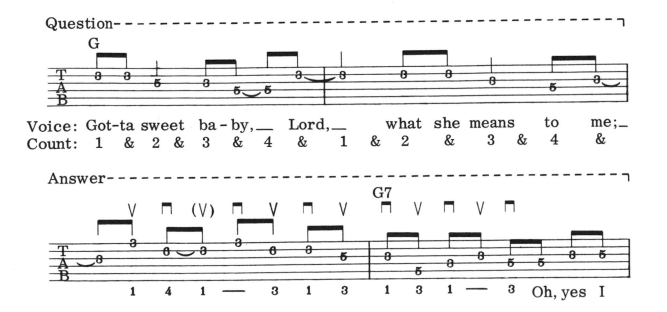

46

Question- -

got-ta sweet ba - by,— Lord, what she means to me;—

Answer- -

3 1 4 1 4 1 4 1 4 1   Oh, yes, and

Question- -

when my ba - by calls me,——— I fall down on my knees.—

Answer- -

3 1 3 1 3 1 3 1 3 Oh, well, I

The primary difference between this and the riff style is that in the riff style the lead is confined to a rhythmic sequence. In the improvised style of the last solo, the lead guitar imitates the human voice. The guitar answers the vocal line with a melody of its own, and this answer is vocal in nature. Many lead guitarists actually sing the lines they are improvising while they are playing!

Two important notes to add to the blues scale:

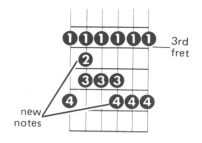

Play this exercise a few times to get these new notes in your fingers.

EXERCISE #2

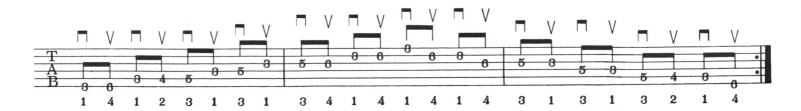

In place of singing the two measure question in the song, substitute an improvised lead part. Now you have an improvised question followed by an improvised answer. You can then play the entire progression as improvisation. It's important, however, to keep in mind that the question phrase is only a *substitution* for the vocal part. This shapes the improvisation. Otherwise, you might play a lot of notes that have little or no meaning. Try this solo:

BLUES IN G #16

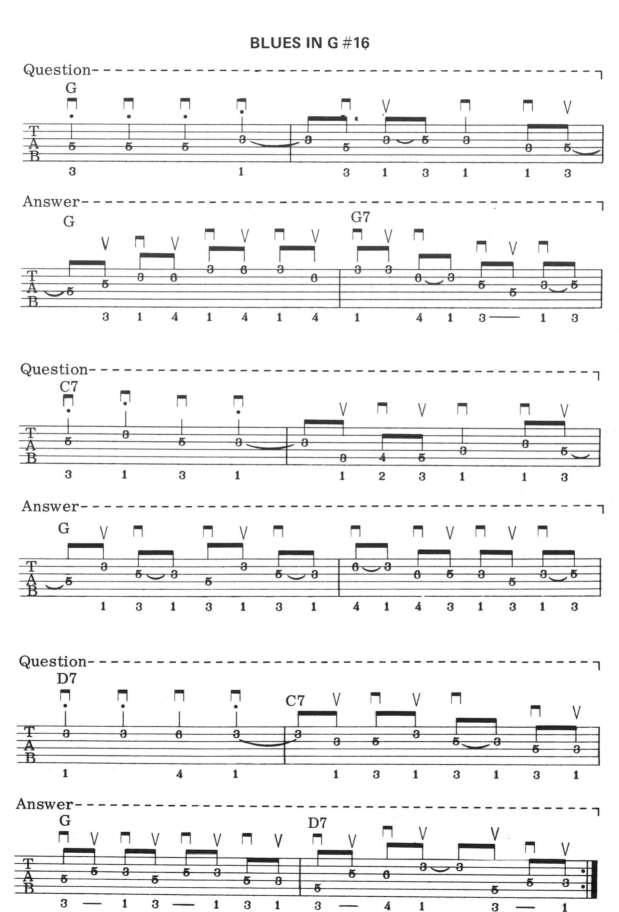

Since the two bar riff has the same number of measures as the question and answer phrases, you can use it for constructing solos in the vocal style. If you consider the first two bar question as the original riff, the following two bar answer could be considered a variation. The next solo illustrates this technique. The last four bars of the progression are frequently melodic riffs played from *root 6 bar chords*.

BLUES IN G #17

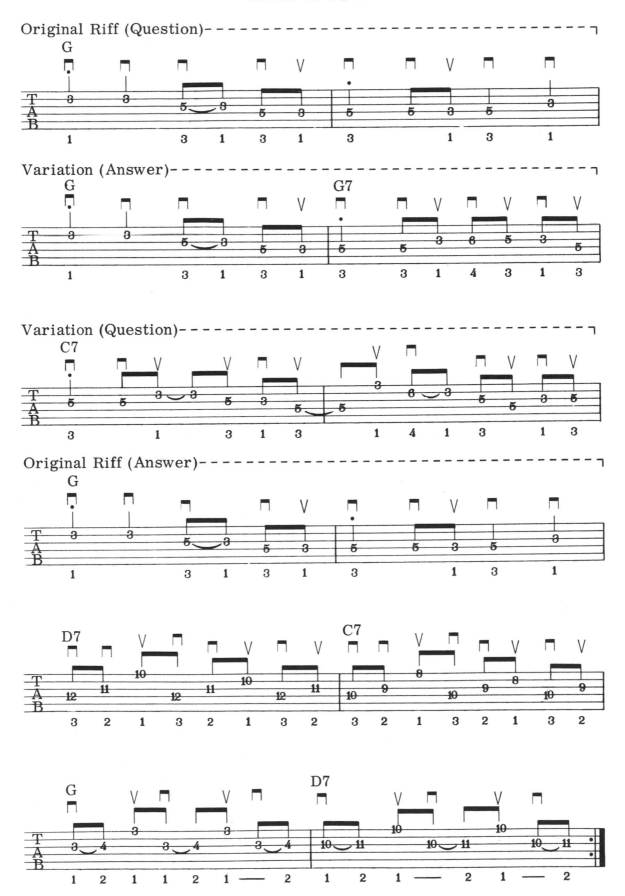

In conclusion, there are several ways to create lead solos. You can improvise lead by using the

1) one measure riff treatment, or the

2) two measure riff treatment, or a

3) two measure vocal style question followed by a two measure vocal style answer, or

4) a combination of the last two.

All four of these improvisational techniques gives form and logic to the solo.

For longer solos, a popular technique is to begin with a chorus using the one measure riff treatment; following that with a chorus using the two measure riff treatment. For the next chorus, improvise in the more flowing vocal style question and answer treatment; then play the second chorus again, and finally end the solo with the first chorus. The solo begins with a tight riff structure and slowly opens in the succeeding choruses; finally, coming back to the original tight riff treatment. Again, the solo has form, logic, excitement, drive and meaning.

The Triplet Trip

Listen to the second side of the record to hear the blues played with a different rhythmic feel (the cut entitled *Triplet Blues in G*). In the counting preceeding the actual playing notice that each beat is subdivided into three parts.

Count: 1 2 3 2 2 3 3 2 3 4 2 3 1

playing begins here

Try counting this new rhythm accenting the first number in each beat.

Using this rhythm you can play three notes or chords on each beat. This figure is called a *triplet* and is notated by three eighth notes with the number "3" written above the connecting beam:

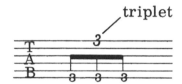

Count and play this example, lightly strumming the G chord three times on each beat.

Count: 1 2 3 2 2 3 3 2 3 4 2 3 1 2 3 2 2 3 3 2 3 4 2 3

The *Triplet Blues in G* also illustrates a popular variation of the standard progression. Analyze the notated outline. Although the same chords are used (G, G7, C7, D7), they change more frequently. This increased number of chord changes suggest more interesting lead lines. Play the progression through a few times using only chords and then try it with the record.

TRIPLET BLUES IN G #1

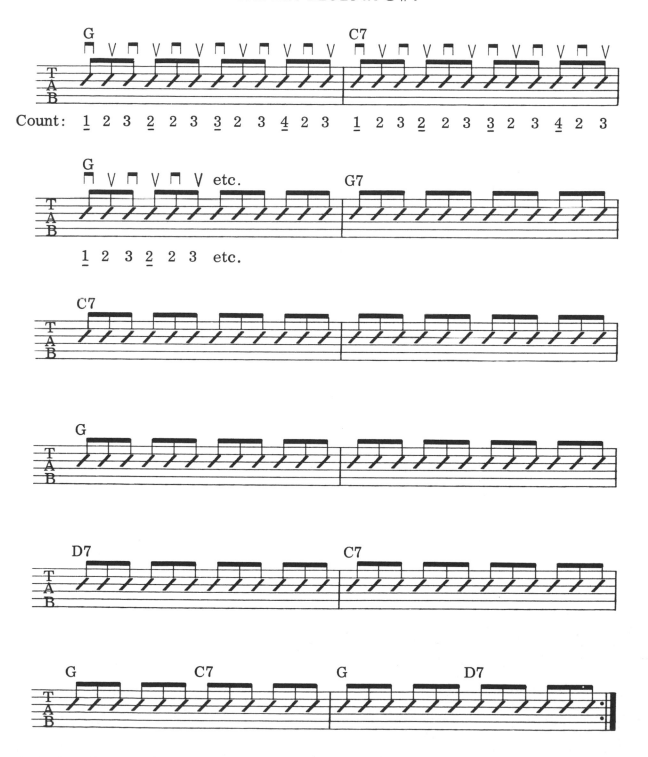

With the exception of the triplet rhythm, this version of the blues progression is quite similar to the one we've been using. (Side One).

Learn this one measure riff in preparation for the first lead solo in triplets. The riff illustrates a rhythmic variation of the one previously learned.

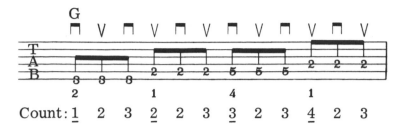

The treatment of the riff in this chordal version of the blues progression is quite similar to the formula you've been using. Since the C7 chord appears in the 2nd measure, switch the riff to the 5th string for that measure. The rest of the progression is handled the same way except in the 11th and 12th measures. Try the solo.

TRIPLET BLUES IN G #2

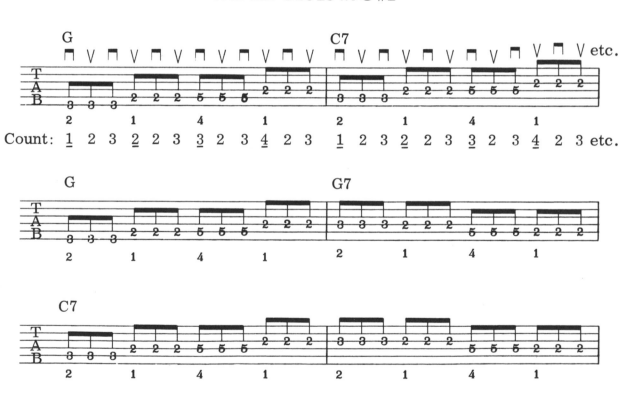

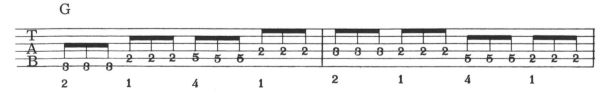

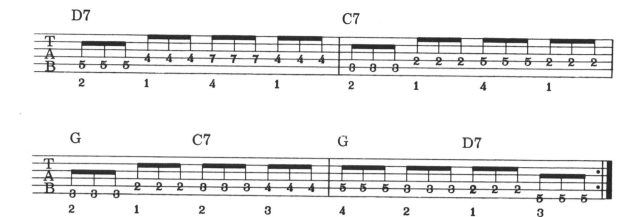

If you had trouble playing the last solo fast enough to accompany the record, work on the next two scale exercises for awhile and then go back to the solo. In any case work on these exercises. They will increase the speed and agility of both your left and right hands. Practice them *very slowly* at first.

EXERCISE #3

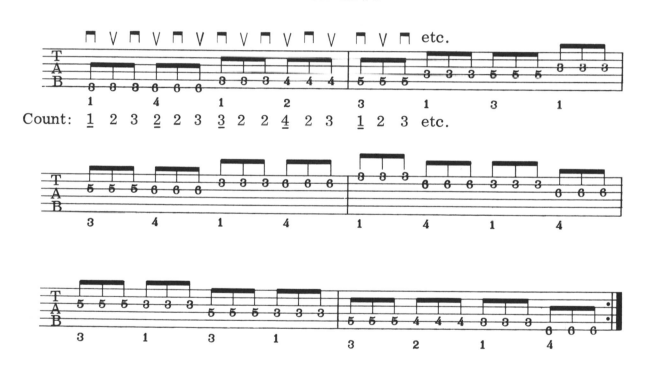

After you've mastered the last exercise, try this one. Play it many times.

EXERCISE #4

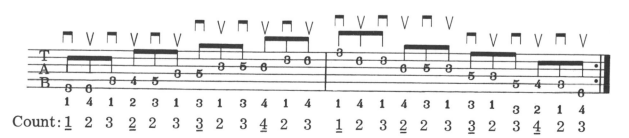

For variation, play the exercises starting with an up-stroke.

EXERCISE #5

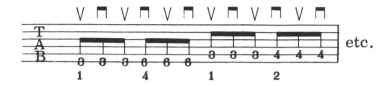

etc.

EXERCISE #6

etc.

These studies are excellent exercises to play before you begin your daily practice. They warm-up your hands and get you in the mood to play.

A very popular rock rhythm based on the triplet is the shuffle rhythm. The shuffle rhythm is achieved by *not playing* on the "2" of the triplet figure. An eighth note rest ⅞ inserted here indicates this rhythm:

To better understand the shuffle rhythm, play the next example. You'll get the feel of this new rhythm quicker if you'll accent the first note of each beat.

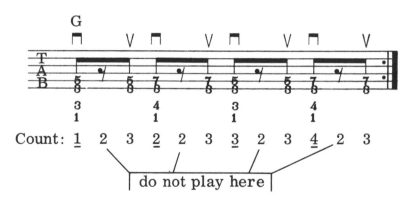

56

After you master this riff (which is a variation of a previous one), play the next solo.
Some of the notes are to be played staccato.

TRIPLET BLUES IN G #3

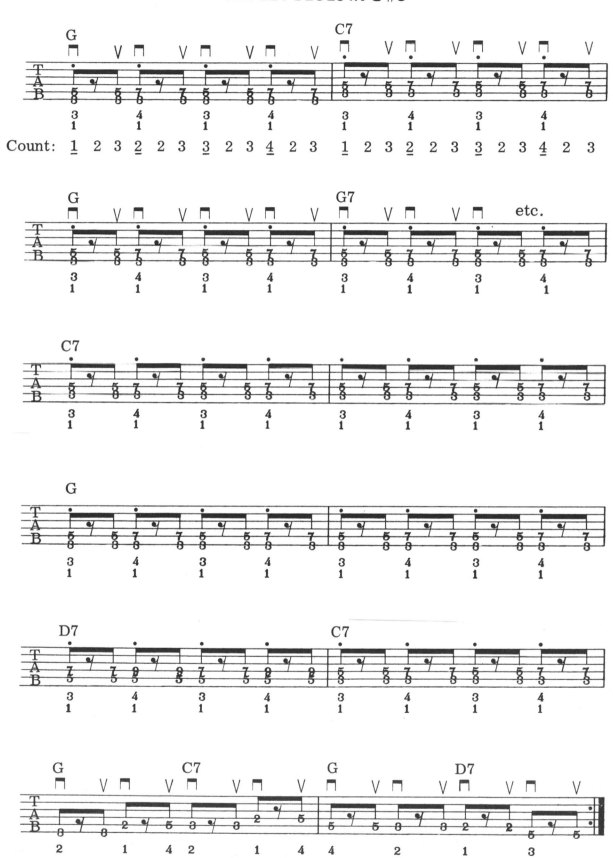

This solo also sounds nice played at a very fast tempo (speed). Try it.

Other eighth note riffs you've learned can be effectively played with the shuffle rhythm. For instance:

EIGHTH NOTE RHYTHM

SHUFFLE RHYTHM

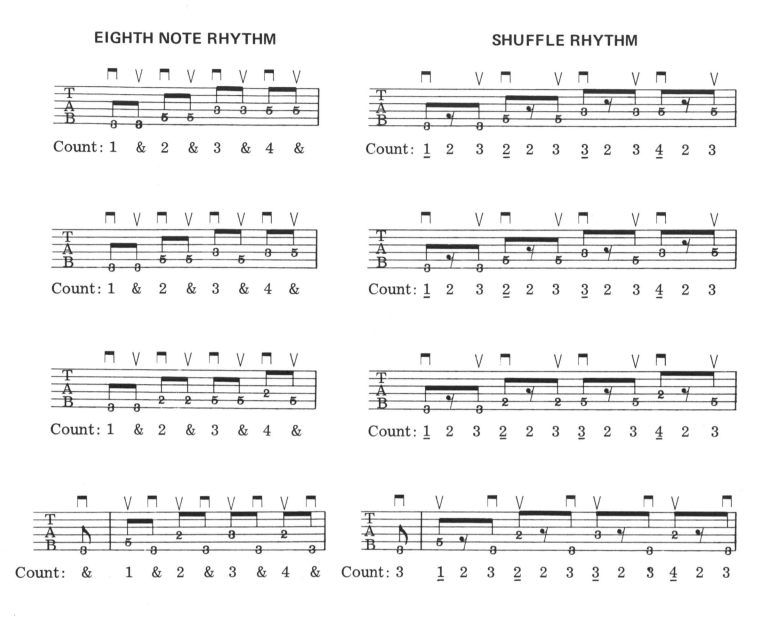

Try a couple of lead solos using some of these shuffle rhythm riffs.

More Blues Scales

When you're improvising lead, it's really beautiful to watch your left hand gliding all over the fingerboard of the guitar like a giant spider twisting, turning, and leaping to new and better riffs. To do this you must have an adequate knowledge of the fingerboard, the guitar, and different ways to play the blues scales.

The G blues scale used up to now is playable starting at other frets of the guitar. For example, you can play this G blues scale with the identical left hand fingering starting at the 15th fret instead of the 3rd fret. It'll take a little practice to get used to playing that high on the fingerboard but this new G blues scale is well worth learning.

G BLUES SCALE

This form of the G blues scale and the earlier form are visually identical, and both scales start with the note G on the 6th string.

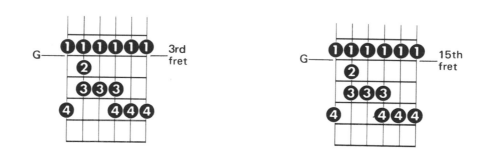

To further familiarize yourself with this new scale, play the two exercises from the previous chapter starting at the 15th rather than the 3rd fret.

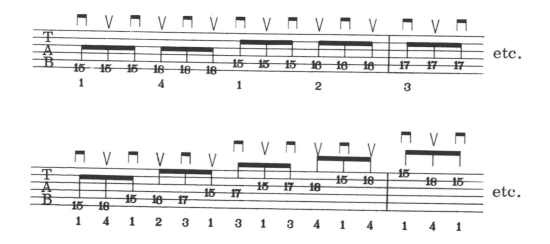

Because of the high pitch of this new scale, straight riff solos are usually not very satisfying. For the most part, this scale should be reserved for vocal type solos. The next solo is from a previous chapter moved up from the 3rd fret G blues scale. (It is to be played with the side one G Blues). How much more intense the same solo becomes when moved to a higher pitch!

BLUES IN G #18

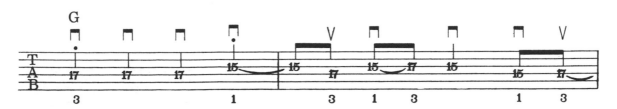

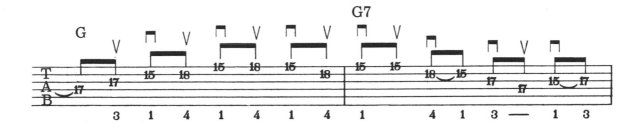

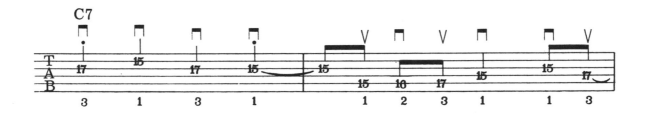

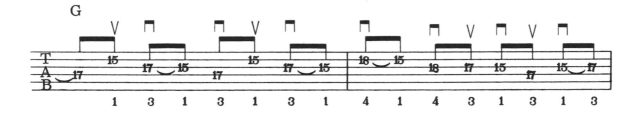

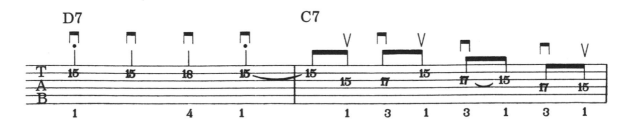

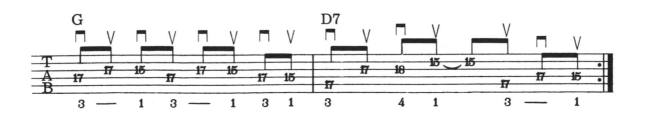

Combining these two scales, an interesting effect can be achieved by starting a lead line on the lower scale and continuing it on the upper one (or vice versa). The question and answer phrases are a natural division for this technique.

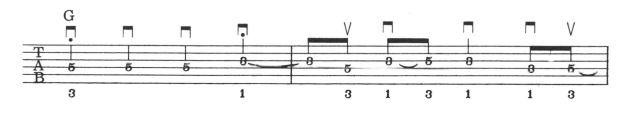

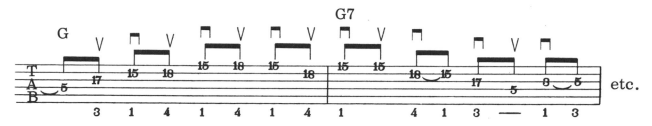

etc.

Since you're now able to play the G blues scale starting at the 3rd fret or starting at the 15th fret, you must imagine you could start the scale at other frets also. You can! First, play the G blues scale on the 6th string alone.

Each one of these notes on the 6th string represent a different starting position for the G blues scale. Since there are only five notes in the blues scale (before they start repeating), the blues scale is playable in five different starting positions. These positions are numbered 1 through 5.

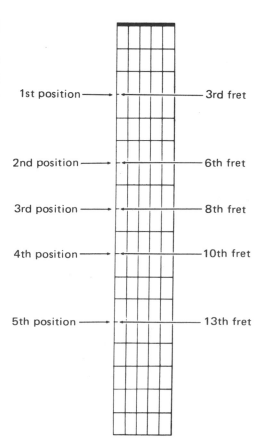

1st position ———→   ——— 3rd fret

2nd position ———→   ——— 6th fret

3rd position ———→   ——— 8th fret

4th position ———→   ——— 10th fret

5th position ———→   ——— 13th fret

The first note in the G blues scale (G) is the starting note for the 1st position scale, the second note starts the 2nd position scale, the third note starts the 3rd position scale, and so forth. The other scale notes on the 6th string are duplicate starting notes.

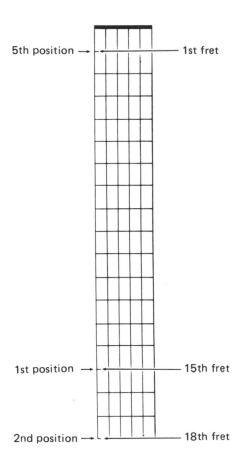

Both the G blues scales we've been working with are 1st position blues scales. The starting note of the lower scale is the 3rd fret of the 6th string. The upper scale starts on the 15th fret of the 6th string. Examine the fingerboard chart to make sure you understand this. The 2nd position G blues scale has its starting note on the 6th fret of the 6th string. Try this:

2nd POSITION G BLUES SCALE

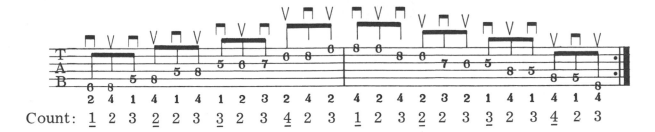

Here's a fingerboard diagram of this scale.

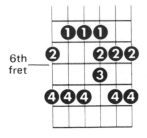

You can also play the 2nd position G blues with the same fingering starting at the 18th fret. Playing the 2nd position scale this high on the fingerboard is impossible unless you're using a single or double cut-away guitar.

2nd POSITION G BLUES SCALE

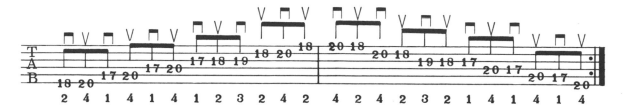

The 1st and 2nd position blues scales are closely related. A solo starting with the 1st position scale is often extended into the 2nd position (and vice versa). Play this next exercise to see how these two scales work together.

EXERCISE #7

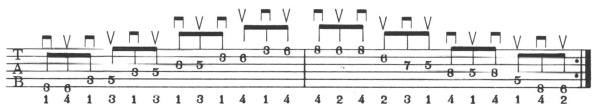

If possible, play the last exercise starting with the upper 1st position G blues scale (15th fret).

The next solo combines the 1st and 2nd position blues scales for a heavy blues lead. The solo is written in the style of Led Zeppelin's lead guitarist Jimmy Page. It begins on the "3" of the 3rd beat and makes much use of the tie.

TRIPLET BLUES IN G #4

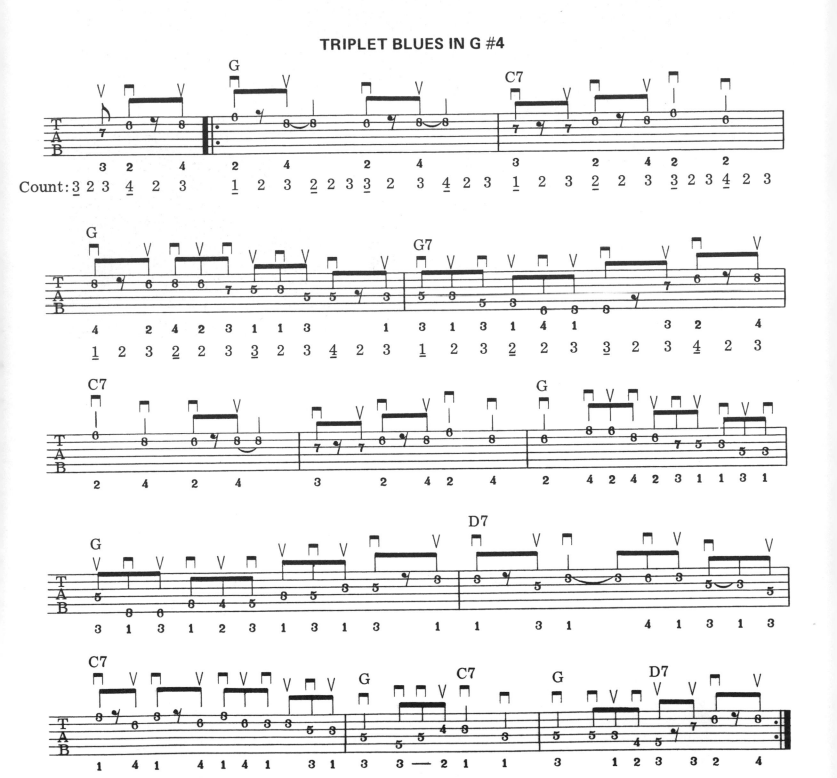

The last solo can also be played using the upper 1st and 2nd position G blues scales. Use the same left hand fingering, the same pick directions, etc. The solo sounds great played this high on the fingerboard.

TRIPLET BLUES IN G #5

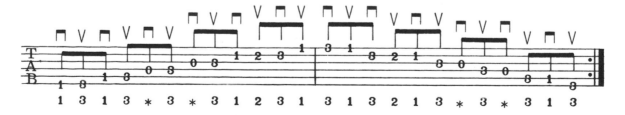

Count: 3 2 3 4 2 3   1 2 3 2 2 3 3 2 3 4 2 3   1 2 3 2 2 3 3 2 3 4 2 3

etc.

Another blues scale frequently used with the 1st position G blues scale is the 5th position scale. It starts at the 1st and the 13th fret of the guitar (examine the fingerboard chart). Try this:

5th POSITION G BLUES SCALE

1 3 1 3 * 3 * 3 1 2 3 1   3 1 3 2 1 3 * 3 * 3 1 3

*An ''o'' indicates an open or unfingered string. No left hand fingering is required.

The fingerboard diagram of this scale looks like this:

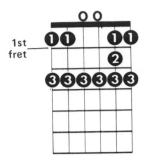

It's easy to locate this scale as it starts immediately below the 1st position scale. After you practice it awhile, try playing the same scale starting at the 13th fret. The fingering is slightly different, so take care.

5th POSITION G BLUES SCALE

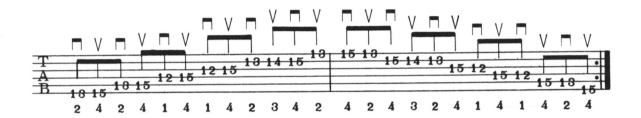

2 4 2 4 1 4 1 4 2 3 4 2   4 2 4 3 2 4 1 4 1 4 2 4

This version of the 5th position blues scale is easy to remember because the pattern is symmetrical. Examine the fingerboard chart.

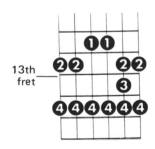

The next solo, which is in the nature of an exercise, illustrates how the 1st, 2nd, and 5th position blues scales function together when playing lead. Practice it slowly at first until you learn it, and then play the solo with the record.

TRIPLET BLUES IN G #6

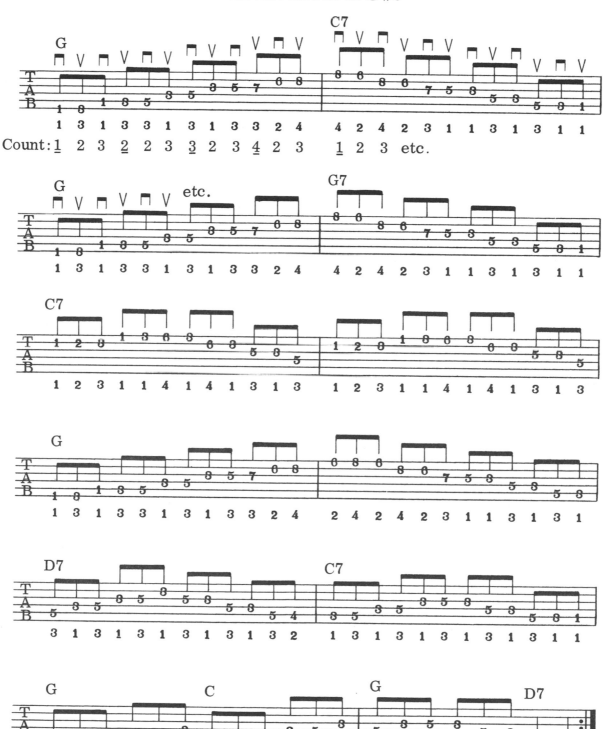

Play the last solo starting with the upper 5th position G blues scale. Use the same left hand fingering, pick directions, etc.

TRIPLET BLUES IN G #7

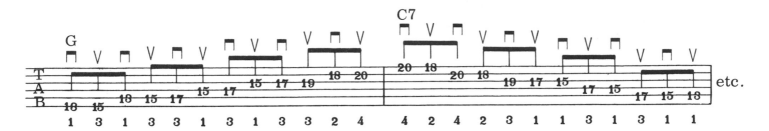

Having successfully completed this chapter, you're on your way to becoming an excellent lead guitarist. It's important, however, to continue practicing the blues scales presented in this lesson. Play both the lower and upper 1st, 2nd, and 5th position blues scales *everyday* before you begin rehearsing or practicing. Every heavy lead guitarist does.

Lay-overs, Slides, and Stuff

Aside from knowing and playing the blues scale when improvising lead, most lead guitarists rely on several instrumental techniques to improve the quality and interest of their playing. One of the more useful of these techniques is the lay-over. *Lay-over* refers to the fingering of two strings by one left hand finger. You'll understand better after playing the next example. Closely follow the drawings above the music leaving the 1st and 3rd fingers in contact with the strings throughout the entire example. The fingering changes result solely from the movement of the last joint of the 3rd finger.

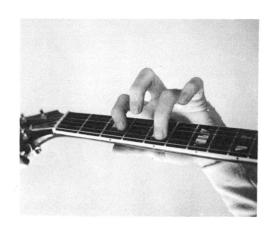

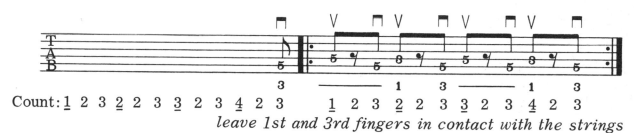

leave 1st and 3rd fingers in contact with the strings

The next exercise further illustrates this technique. It's a very useful exercise so spend some time on it.

LAY-OVER EXERCISE

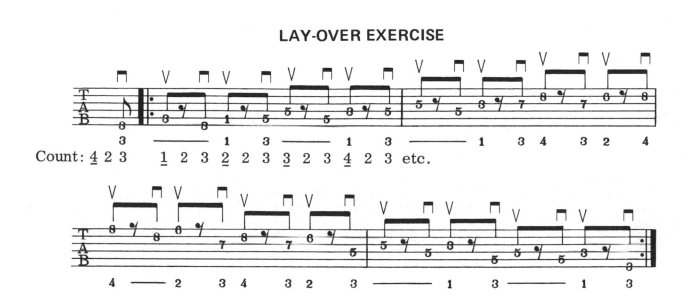

69

After you can play the last exercise at a pretty fast speed, try the next solo written in the style of the Door's guitarist Robby Krieger. It is a riff type solo and makes much use of the lay-over.

TRIPLET BLUES IN G #8

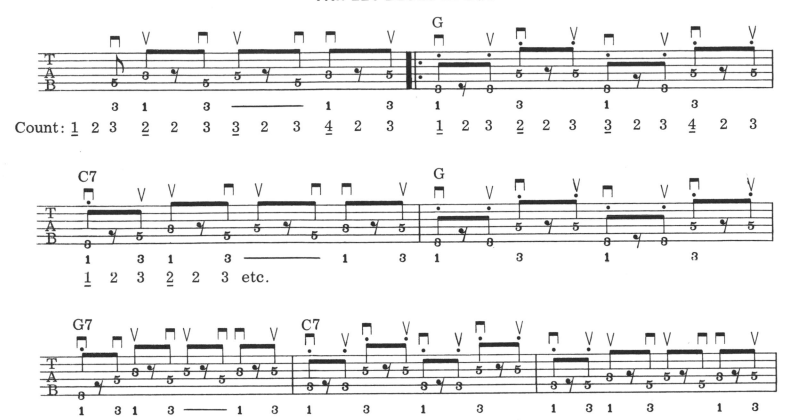

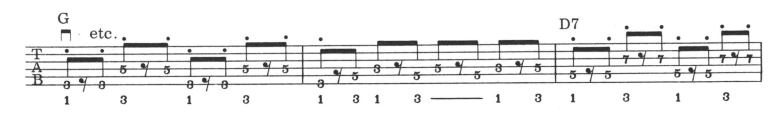

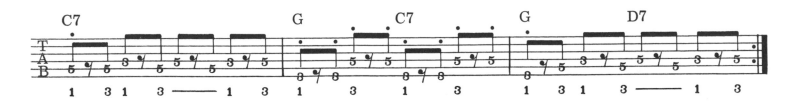

Another popular lead technique is the *slide*, indicated by a straight line ⟋
When two notes are connected by the slide marking, play the first note at the
indicated fret. While the note is still ringing, produce the next note by quickly
sliding to it *without* plucking the string again. In this example, play the 3rd string at
the 5th fret then, while that note is still ringing, slide up to the next note at the 7th
fret. Leave the 3rd finger in contact with the string throughout the example.

The reverse of this is to first play the 3rd string at the 7th fret then, while the note is
still ringing, slide down to the lower note causing it to ring. Again, leave the 3rd
finger in contact with the string throughout the example.

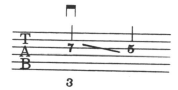

Try this short exercise which illustrates the more common slides.

SLIDE EXERCISE #1

Slides are often combined with snap-offs and hammer-ons. Here's the last exercise
using all three techniques.

SLIDE EXERCISE #2

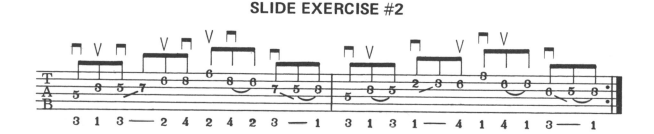

Now for a solo. If the snap-offs and hammer-ons give you lots of trouble, play the solo using only the slides at first. After you have the slides in your fingers, add the snap-offs and hammer-ons.

TRIPLET BLUES IN G #9

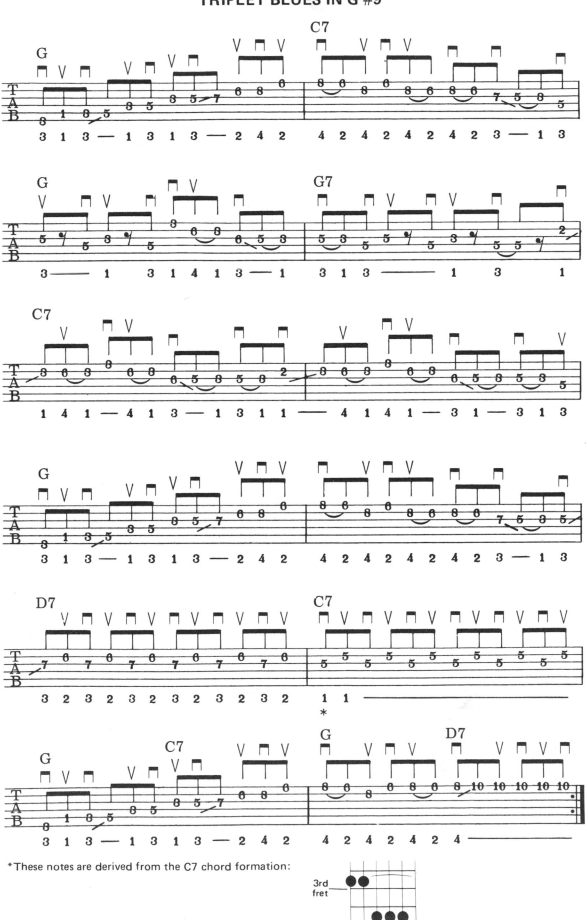

*These notes are derived from the C7 chord formation:

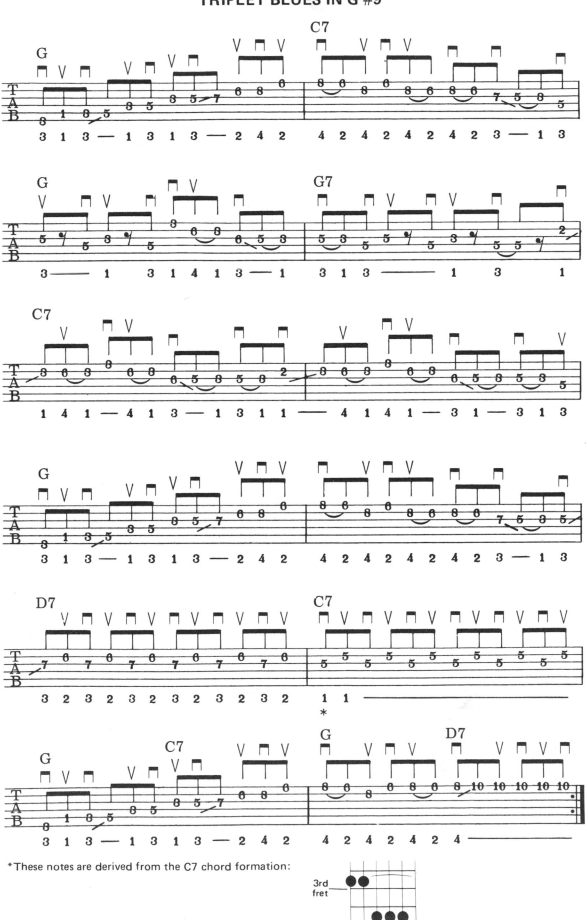

3rd fret

A jagged line going either up ⌇⌇ or down ⌇⌇ after a note indicates a slide to an indefinite pitch. In this example, play the 1st string at the 5th fret and immediately slide up the fingerboard releasing your finger at the 8th fret or so.

Sliding down is just the opposite.

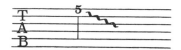

This type of slide is usually employed at the end of a short melodic phrase. Here's an example in an excerpt from our solo on page 49.

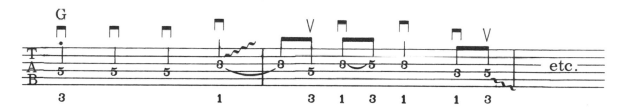

Another frequently used lead technique is the *bend.* The bend is indicated by a wavy line ⌇ over a note and is played by pushing the string toward you with considerable pressure.* This stretches the string and causes it to go up in pitch:

or

*The bend is quite easy to execute with light-gauge strings.

In the next example, play the 3rd string at the 5th fret. As soon as you play the string, push the fretting finger towards you, raising the pitch. The number in parentheses indicates to what note the string is bent to. The sound produced by the bend is similar to that produced by the slide.

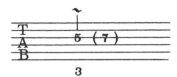

The reverse of this is to first bend the string and as soon as you play it, relax the finger. This results in a lowering of pitch.

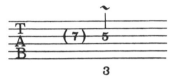

When the number in parentheses follows the bent note, bend up to that pitch. When the number in parentheses comes before the bent note, bend down from that pitch. In both examples, finger only the 5th fret of the 3rd string. Often both types of bends are used together.

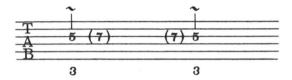

Bringing these new techniques together for a heavy lead: This solo is written in the style of the great blues singer and guitarist, Aaron T. Bone Walker. One of the grand-daddies of blues guitar, he was laying down some together-leads even before the Depression. T. Bone's style has influenced generations of singers and guitarists!

TRIPLET BLUES IN G #10

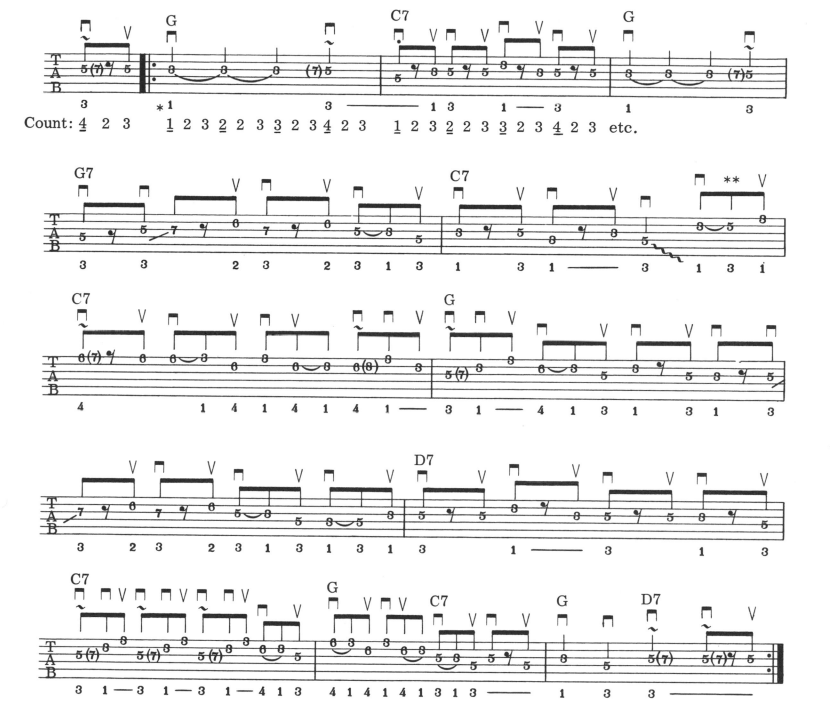

*Here's another use of the tie: sustain the note thru the first three beats.

**This note also belongs to the C7 chord. More about this later.

And More Blues Scales

Two other important blues scales to know are the 3rd and 4th position blues scales. By learning these last two positional scales, you will be able to improvise lead from virtually any place on the fingerboard. Examine and play this 4th position G blues scale.

4th POSITION G BLUES SCALE

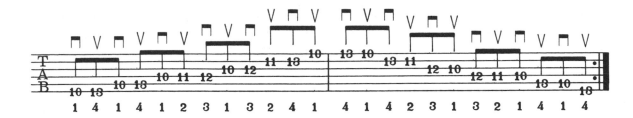

The fingerboard diagram looks like this:

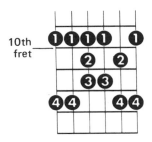

To further familiarize yourself with this scale, play the triplet exercise.

TRIPLET EXERCISE

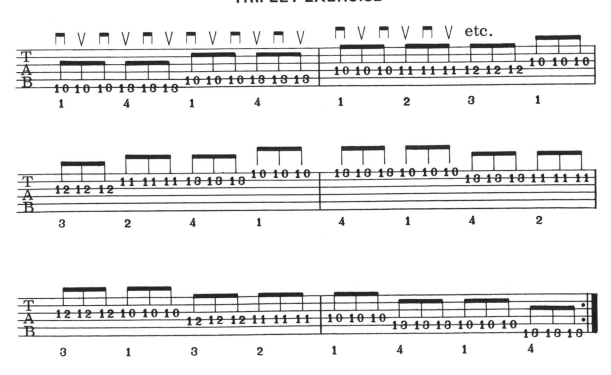

The 4th position blues scale is an extremely useful scale. Complete lead solos are often played using only this scale. Before we get into one, pick up on a new note value. First, play a few bars of the last exercise:

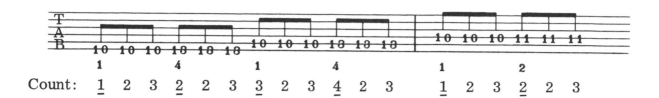

Subdivide each beat of the triplet figure by inserting "a" between each number: 1-a-2-a-3-a 2-a-2-a-3-a 3-a-2-a-3-a 4-a-2-a-3-a. Play a note on each syllable. This is the sixteenth note rhythm which is indicated by a double beam.

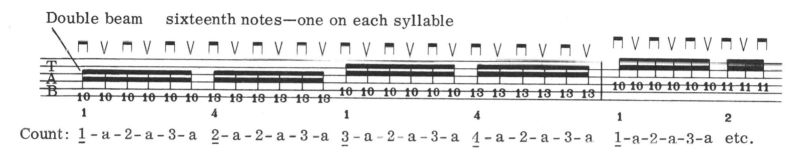

Sixteenth and eighth notes are often mixed when playing triplet figures. The next two exercises illustrate the more popular mixtures. Count and play them very slowly at first until you get a feel for them. In the first exercise play two sixteenth notes on each beat.

EXERCISE #8

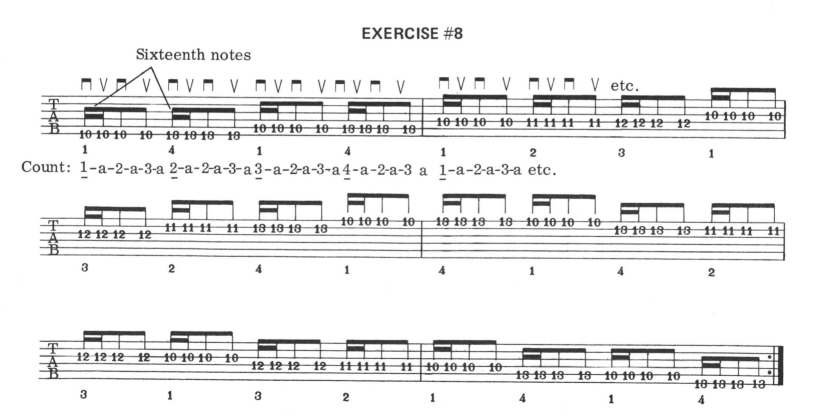

In this exercise, play two sixteenth notes *before* each beat.

EXERCISE #9

Count: 1-a-2-a-3-a 2-a-2-a-3-a 3-a-2-a-3-a 4-a-2-a-3-a 1-a-2-a-3-a 2-a-2-a-3-a etc.

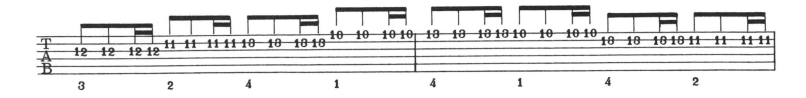

For further practice, play these two exercises using the 1st position blues scale.

A solo to illustrate how to use the 4th position blues scale when playing lead. The solo is written in the style of the great lead guitarist and blues singer, Albert King. One of the characteristics of Albert King's style is the frequent insertion of sixteenth notes just before and on the beat.

TRIPLET BLUES IN G #11

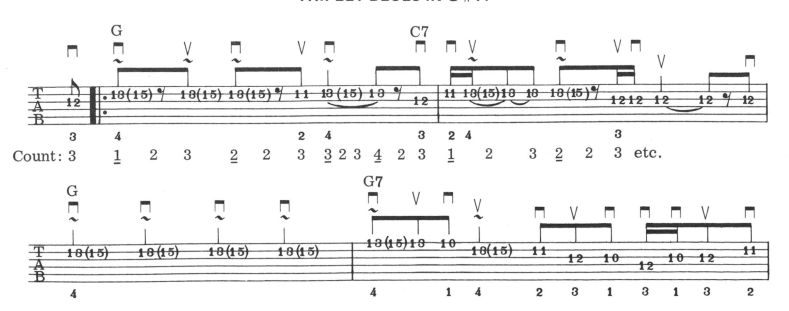

Count: 3   1   2   3   2   2   3 3 2 3 4 2 3   1   2   3   2   2   3 etc.

78

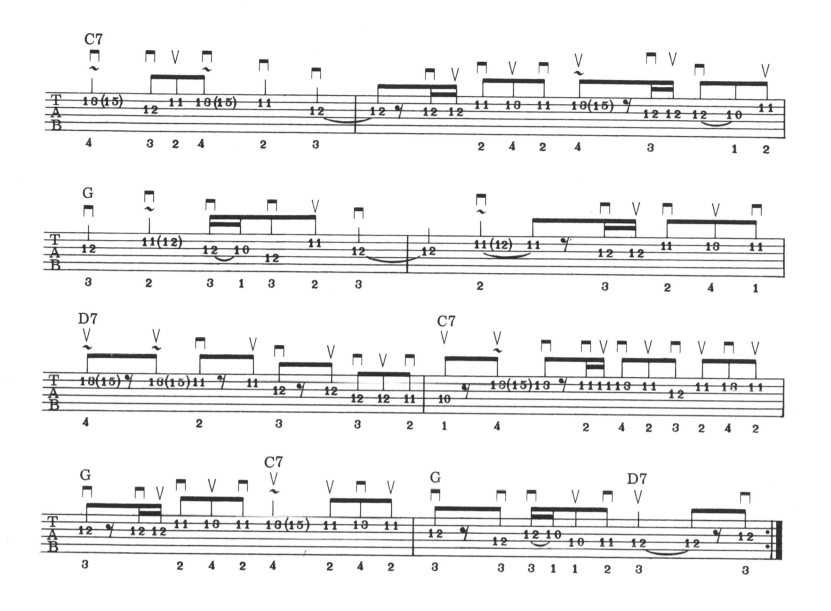

The last positional blues scale to learn is the 3rd position scale.

3rd POSITION G BLUES SCALE

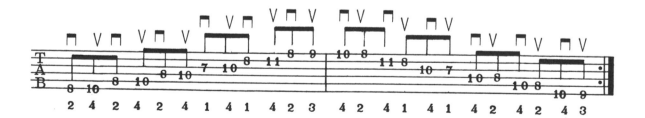

The fingerboard diagram:

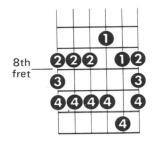

The 3rd and 4th position blues scales are often played together when improvising. The next solo, which is in the nature of an exercise, illustrates the more common lay-overs, slides, and hammer-ons used when playing in these two scales.

TRIPLET BLUES IN G #12

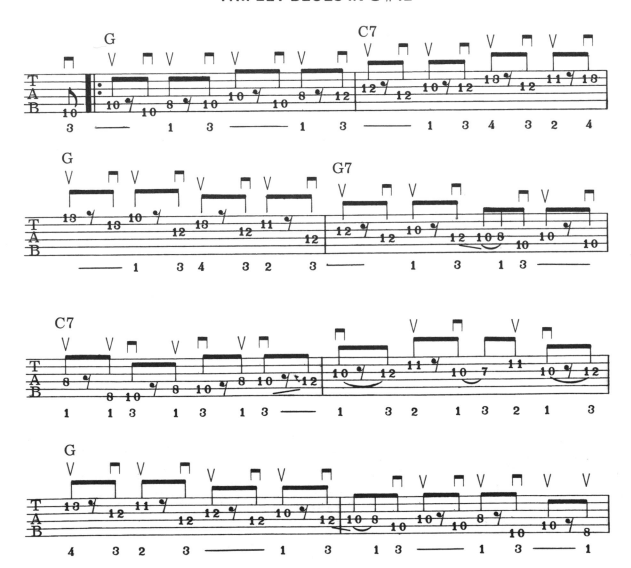

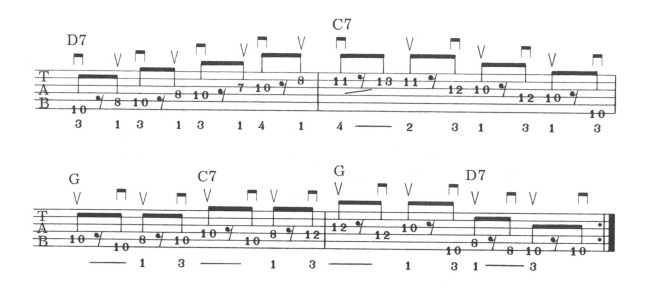

Now that you know all five positions of the G blues scale, practice them daily. When you're improvising, no matter where you are on the fingerboard of the guitar a blues scale lies below your fingers. Any type of blues line can be played if you really know these scales.

Advanced Effects

The single technique that contributes the most to today's lead sound is the *tremolo* (also called the *vibrato*). Strictly speaking, to play a tremolo means to cause a note to vary quickly up and down in pitch, creating a sound similar to the human voice. There are several ways to product a tremolo: the easiest is by using the tremolo (or whammy) bar. First play a note and then bring the tremolo bar into play. A wavy line 〰 over the note* indicates this technique:

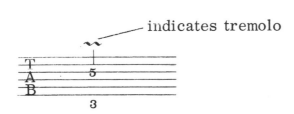

tremolo bar

There are two methods of obtaining the tremolo effect without using the mechanical tremolo bar.** You should be familiar with them. Both of these methods rely on moving the sounding string from side to side causing the pitch to go up and down.

The first method is the *finger tremolo.* It is achieved by moving the tip-end of the fretting finger towards the palm of the hand (the opposite of the bend), and then back to its original position. The idea is to move the finger-tip rapidly back and forth.

natural position

index finger pulling toward palm

back to natural position

*This is the same sign used for the bend. Without the note in parentheses, the bend sign indicates a tremolo.

**Many lead guitarists refuse to equip their guitars with tremolo bars arguing that the tremolo bar causes the guitar to go out of tune and that it is a mechanical and therefore not a natural effect. It will cause slight tuning problems but there are many advantages: you can tremolo feedback, chords, and extremely high notes on the guitar that would be impossible without the tremolo bar. Also, the country and western slide guitar effect can be simulated by using a tremolo bar (Bigsby is the preferred tremolo tailpiece).

This method works on every string with the exception of the 1st. For the 1st string, use either the tremolo bar or the bend.

Another method is the *wrist tremolo* and is achieved by rotating the wrist causing the entire hand to move. By leaving the fretting finger stationary and moving the hand, an excellent tremolo is obtained.

 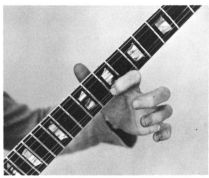 

regular position of the wrist   wrist rotating   wrist back to regular position

With any method of tremolo, the note must be sustained for the tremolo to be effective. This is achieved by installing extra-sensitive pick-ups on your guitar (Humbucker Pick-ups are preferred by many guitarists).

Try the next exercise to help you master the tremolo. Use either the finger or the wrist tremolo. The tremolo is not an easy effect to achieve. Practice it slowly.

TREMOLO EXERCISE

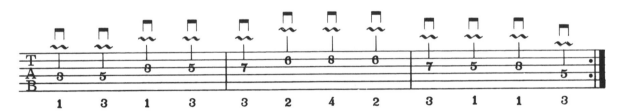

For further practice, play the tremolo with all positions of the blues scale. It will take a lot of practice to master this technique. Here's an excerpt from our solo illustrating when the tremolo is used. Notice that the tremolo is used on the longer note values and for phrase endings.

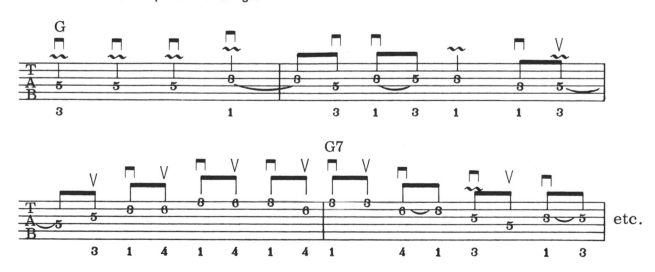

Another effective sound is the *double bend.* The double bend is achieved by fingering two strings and bending one of them. Finger these two strings.

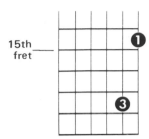

Bend the 2nd string while leaving the 1st string unbent. If you have trouble bending so far, use the 2nd finger to assist the bending finger.

The idea is for both strings to produce the same pitch. A wavy line *below* the lowest string indicates this effect.

This effect is generally used high on the fingerboard because of the great distance of the 2nd string bend. The sound produced by the double bend is quite strong and should be preserved for special situations. Other double bends can be found in the next solo.

Still another effect is the grace note technique. This effect is achieved by playing a note and instantly snapping off the fretting finger producing a lower note. The grace note ornaments the main note, and its time value is as short as possible. The grace note is played on the beat and is usually notated in small type.

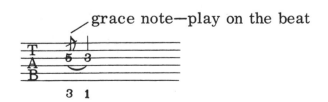

Play the lower note first and instantly hammer on the upper note for another type of grace note. As before, the grace note is played on the beat.

A grace note can also be achieved by playing the lower note and quickly sliding to the upper one.

Or vice versa:

A short exercise illustrating all four types of grace notes. The exercise has to be played quite fast to sound good. Remember to play all grace notes on the beat.

A SHORT EXERCISE

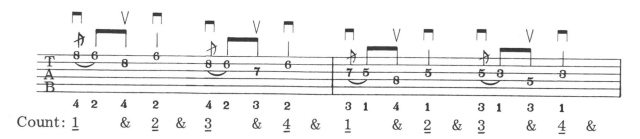

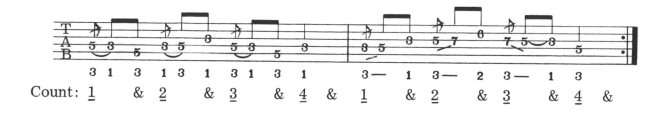

The next solo is written in the style of the talented lead guitarist Alvin Lee of the group Ten Years After. It is a difficult solo full of grace notes and slides and double bends and sixteenth notes and all kinds of nice and exciting things. For the most part, this type if intricate lead work is reserved for very slow blues and rock tunes—practice this blues at about half the speed of the *Triplet Blues in G* on side two.

TRIPLET BLUES IN G #13

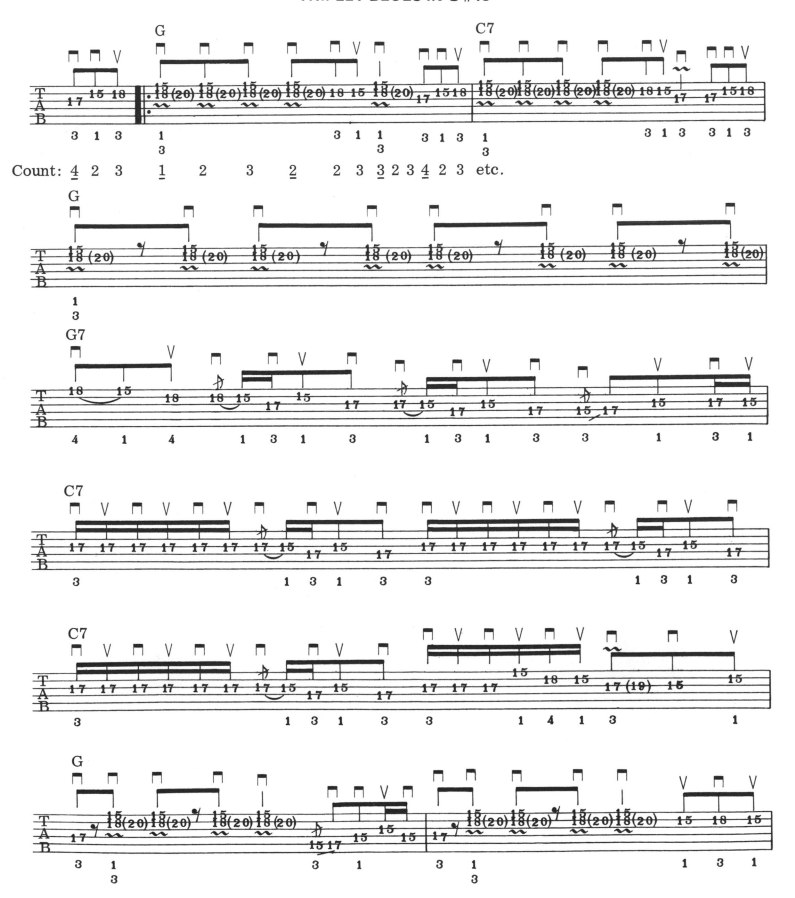

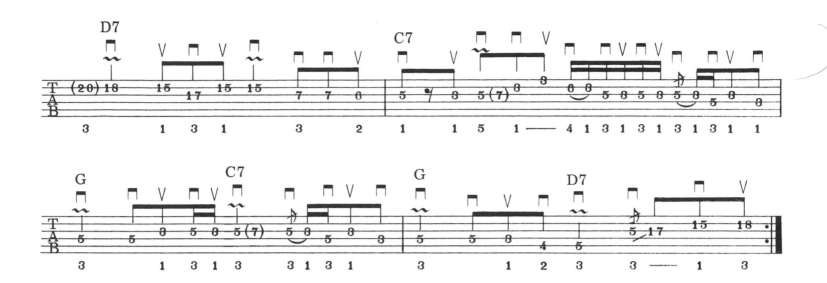

Modulation

By now you might think that all rock songs consist of a blues progression played in the key of G. Although G is a favorite key for blues lead, there are several other common blues keys. To begin with, the key of a blues progression is determined by the first chord in the progression. In the G blues progression the first chord is G. In the chord structure of an A blues progression the first chord is A.

BLUES IN A

Play the chords to the blues progression in A simply by moving the chords from the G blues progression *up* two frets.

G Blues Chords

A Blues Chords

G

A

moved up two frets becomes

G7

A7

moved up two frets becomes

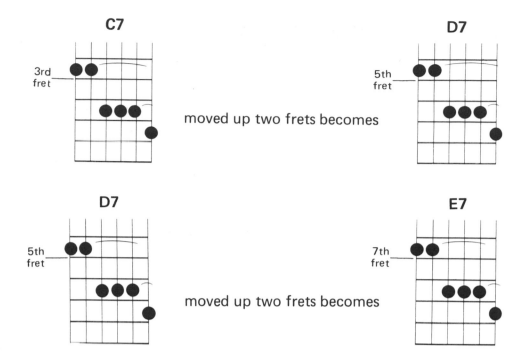

C7 ... moved up two frets becomes **D7**

3rd fret / 5th fret

D7 ... moved up two frets becomes **E7**

5th fret / 7th fret

By knowing the notes produced by the 6th string, you can play the blues progression chords in any key. When you start the progression with the first chord behind the 3rd fret (the 3rd fret of the 6th string produces the note G) the progression is in the key of G. When the first chord is behind the 5th fret (the 6th string produces the note A) the progression is in the key of A. Behind the 8th fret the key is C; behind the 10th fret the key is D; behind the 12th fret the key is E. Play the chord structure for the blues progression in these common keys (A, C, D, and E). Do it!

BLUES IN C

C /F7 /C /C7 /F7 /F7 /C /C /G7 /F7 /C F7/C G7//
8th fret

BLUES IN D

D /G7 /D /D7 /G7 /G7 /D /D /A7 /G7 /D G7/D A7//
10th fret

BLUES IN E

E /A7 /E /E7 /A7 /A7 /E /E /B7 /A7 /E A7/E B7//
12th fret

Locating the blues scales in these new keys is also determined by the notes produced by the 6th string. The 1st position G blues scale is played starting at the 3rd fret of the 6th string which produces the note G. To locate the starting note of the 1st position A blues scale, find A on the 6th string (5th fret) and start the scale at that fret. Use the same left hand fingering for all 1st position scales.

1st POSITION BLUES SCALE IN A

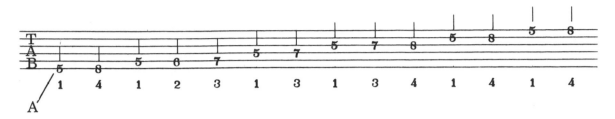

The 1st position C blues scale starts at the 8th fret:

1st POSITION BLUES SCALE IN C

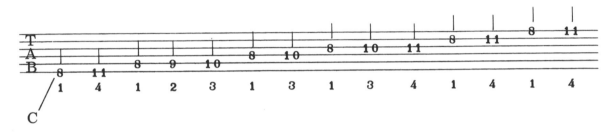

The 1st position D blues scale starts at the 10th fret:

1st POSITION BLUES SCALE IN D

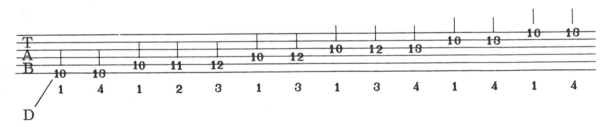

The 1st position E blues scale starts at the 12th fret:

1st POSITION BLUES SCALE IN E

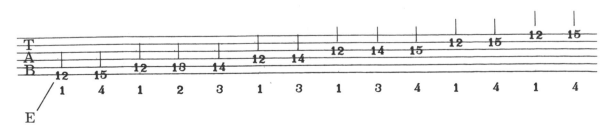

Another important 1st position E blues scale can be played using open strings. Because of the open strings, the left hand fingering is slightly different.

1st POSITION BLUES SCALE IN E

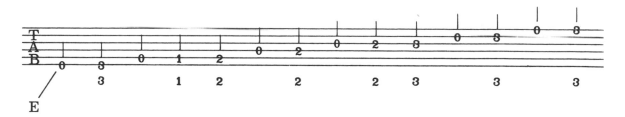

To make sure you understand these new scales, play them using the triplet exercises.

The other positional blues scales can easily be located once you determine the starting fret for the 1st position blues scale. If the 1st position A blues scale is located two frets above the 1st position G blues scale, likewise all the other G blues scales are moved up two frets for the key of A.

**2nd Position
Blues Scale In G**

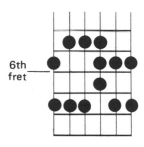

6th fret

moved up two frets becomes

**2nd Position
Blues Scale In A**

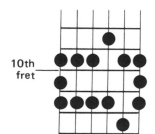

8th fret

**3rd Position
Blues Scale In G**

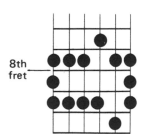

8th fret

moved up two frets becomes

**3rd Position
Blues Scale In A**

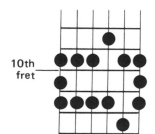

10th fret

Follow the same procedure to transfer the other G blues scales to the key of A. Here's a fingerboard reference for the key of A giving all the starting notes for the different positional blues scales:

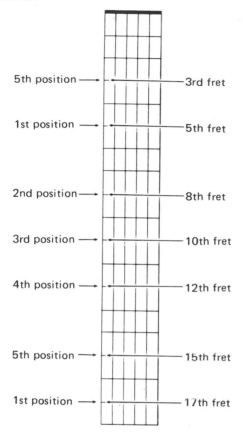

Practice the blues scales in all five positions using the triplet exercises.

Here are the starting notes for the blues scales in the key of C. Practice them in all five positions also.

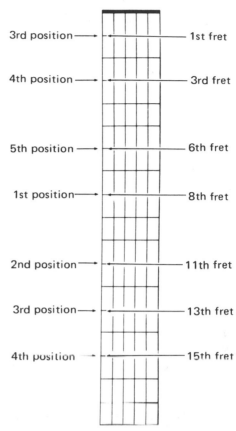

The starting notes for the key of D:

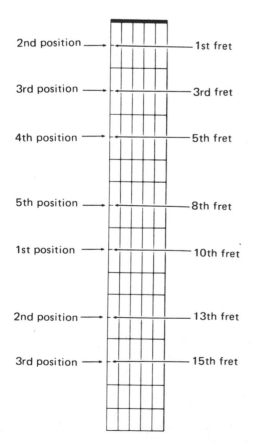

The starting notes for the key of E:

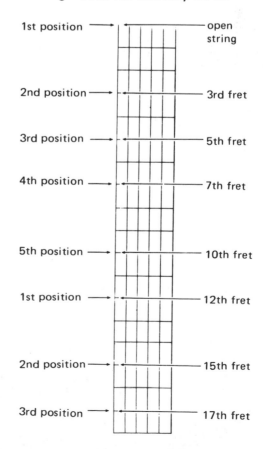

You should be thoroughly familiar with all positions of the blues scale in these important keys. You can easily spend a week learning all five positions in each key (and a lifetime playing them). Any exercise notated in G can be transferred (transposed) to one of these new keys. You can go through the entire book playing everything in the key of A, or the key of C, or the key of D, etc. Try recording the blues rhythm background of the new key on a tape recorder and playing the solos with the recording. Here's an excerpt of a solo originally written in the key of G and moved up to A. Play the solo with the same fingering, pick directions, phrasing, and so on. The solo is just played two frets higher than the original.

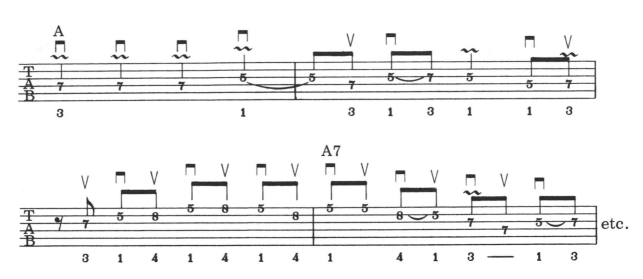

To play the same solo in the key of C, simply move the solo up three more frets.

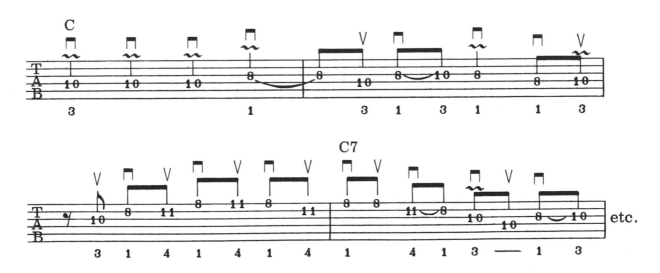

Follow the same procedure to transpose any other solo or exercise.

Other Rock Scales

Although most rock songs fit the 12 bar blues progression or a progression derived from it, there are many other chord progressions for rock songs. A knowledge of a few additional scales and ornamental patterns will equip you to improvise in any song. A very important scale to learn is the 6th scale. Try this G 6th scale played in triplet rhythm.

G 6th SCALE

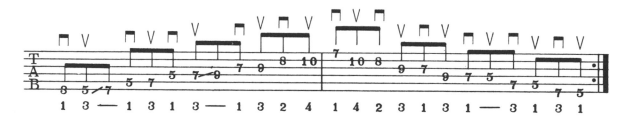

The first note of the 6th scale determines the letter name of the scale as well as the chord that it can be used to improvise with. The first note of this 6th scale is G (3rd fret of the 6th string) so it is a G 6th scale. With this scale you can improvise with any G (or G7) chord.

By starting the 6th scale at the 8th fret, you can play a C 6th scale (the first note is now C). Use the same fingering and pick directions as with the G 6th scale.

C 6th SCALE

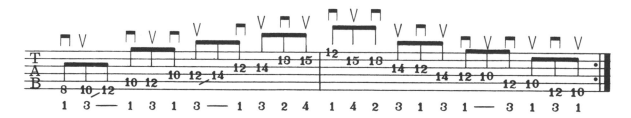

The C 6th scale can be used to improvise with any C or C7 chord.

Starting the scale at the 10th fret gives you a D 6th scale:

D 6th SCALE

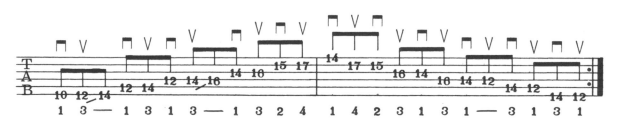

Remember, when using a 6th scale the letter name of the 6th scale and the chord that you're improvising against must be the same (use the G 6th scale with a G or G7 chord, the C 6th scale with a C or C7 chord, etc.). The next solo illustrates some popular soul and R & B lead riffs derived from the 6th scales. Play the solo with side one of the record.

BLUES IN G #19

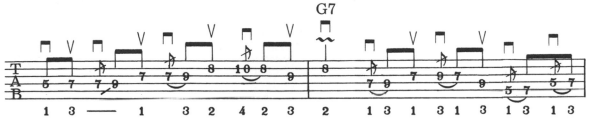

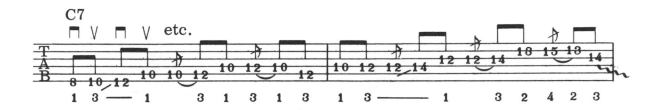

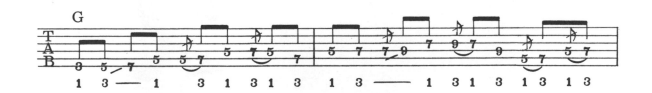

Another important rock scale is the Memphis scale. Popular with soul* band lead guitarists it is well worth learning. One of its characteristics is that you play the 1st and 3rd strings together without sounding the 2nd string. Finger these two strings with the left hand:

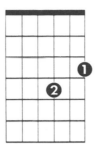

Play the 3rd string with the pick and the 1st string with the middle finger of the right hand. Sound both the 3rd and 1st strings simultaneously.

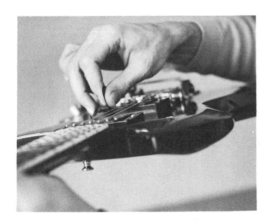

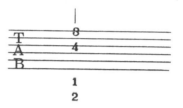

The scale also uses the 2nd and 4th strings together while skipping the 3rd string:

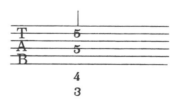

Now try the G Memphis scale:

G MEMPHIS SCALE #1

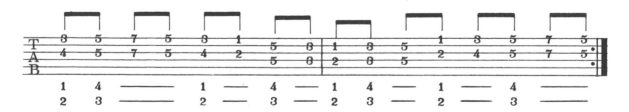

*Much of the music associated with the soul sound is recorded in studios located in Memphis which accounts for the name of this scale.

Like the 6th scale, the Memphis scale can only be used to improvise with the chord that has the same letter name as the scale. The G Memphis scale is used to improvise with any G or G7 chord. Since the first two notes of the Memphis scale are part of the *root 6 bar chord,* this chord determines the letter name of the scale as well as the chord with which this scale can be used.

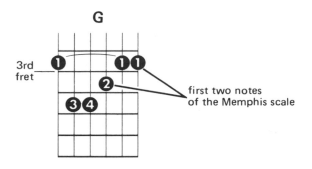

The C Memphis scale is played starting at the 8th fret (the C chord is located at the 8th fret). This scale illustrates a variation in the rhythm of the Memphis scale. The top string can be played with either the middle finger or the pick.

C MEMPHIS SCALE

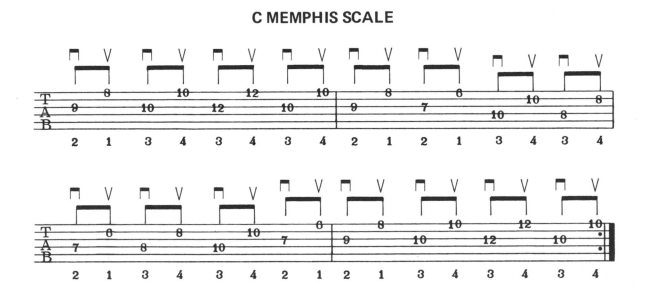

The D Memphis scale is played starting at the 10th fret:

D MEMPHIS SCALE

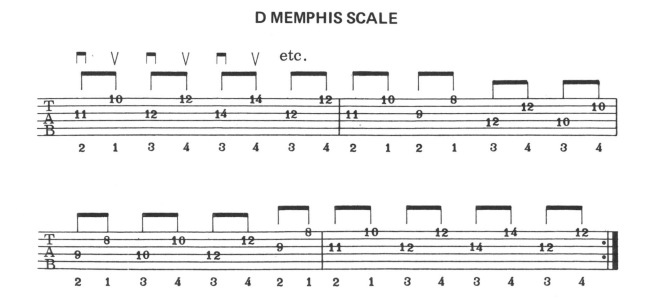

The next blues solo illustrates some of the popular lead riffs derived from the Memphis scale. Play this solo with the blues on side two of the record.

TRIPLET BLUES IN G #14

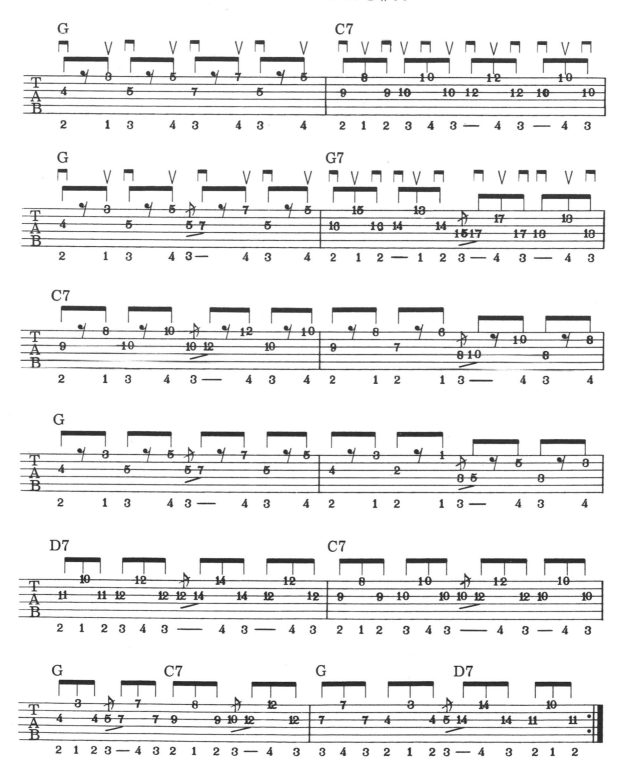

By raising the 2nd finger of the left hand, the *root 6 bar chord* you've been using becomes a minor chord.

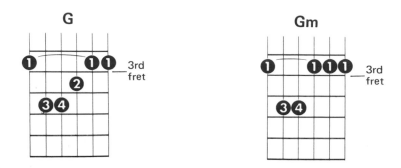

Strum both chords and listen to the difference. The G minor chord has a empty, melancholy sound that the G chord does not have. To finger any minor chord first locate the *root 6 bar chord* of the same letter name and simply raise the 2nd finger (the C chord changes to a Cm chord, the D chord to Dm, etc.). Practice changing some of the *root 6 bar chords* you know into minor chords.

When a minor chord appears in a chord progression, use the blues scale of the same letter name to improvise with. For example, to improvise with a G minor chord (Gm or Gm7) use the G blues scale.

Another scale used to improvise with minor chords is the jazz minor scale.

G MINOR JAZZ SCALE

The first note of the jazz scale on the 6th string determines the letter name of the scale and the minor chord it can be used to improvise with. To play the minor jazz scale in A, start the scale at the 5th fret of the 6th string. Use this scale to improvise with any Am or Am7 chord.

100

A MINOR JAZZ SCALE

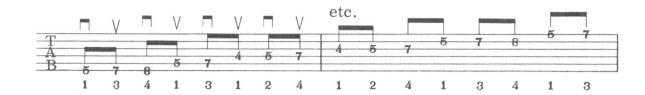

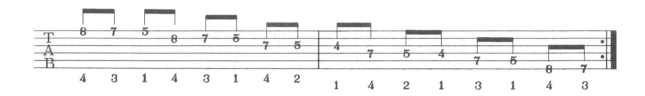

Solos using the jazz minor scale have a very flowing and non-urgent nature. Dreamy ragas and jazz-like lines can be played when improvising with this scale. The next progression provides a chord background for such a solo using the A minor jazz scale. Although G chords appear in the progression, the Am chords played at the beginning of each measure give the progression an A minor flavor. Try just playing the chords first:

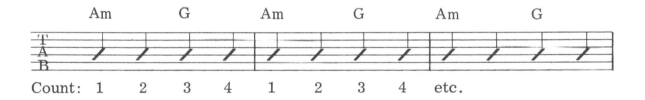

And the solo. Once you get into this style of playing, you can create solos that drift
on and on and on. Just remember to play only the A minor jazz scale.

SOLO IN A MINOR

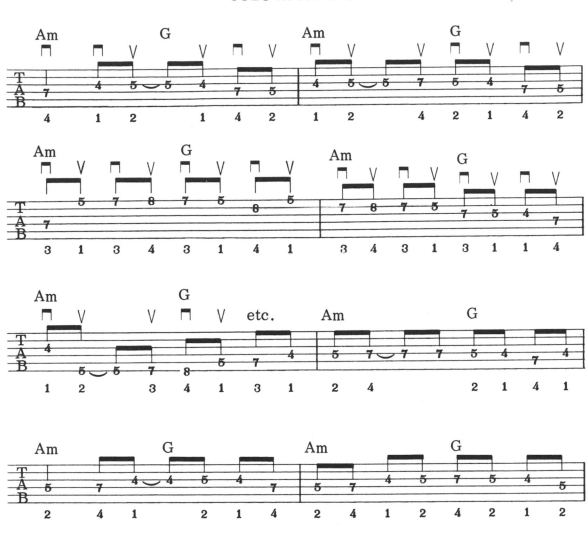

Another lead figure used with minor chords is the *bounce.* The bounce consists of
two grace notes—a combination of a hammer-on followed by a snap-off. Only the
first note is played with the pick with the other two sounded by the left hand. Try
this:

When playing the bounce with the minor chord, finger only the first four strings like so:

Gm

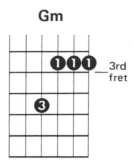

With the G minor chord thus fingered, play the hammer-ons and snap-offs with the left hand pinky.

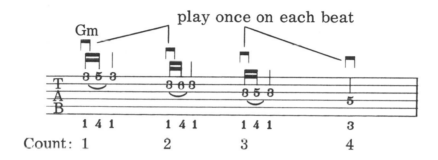

To play the bounce with the regular *root 6 bar chord*, finger only the first four strings also:

G

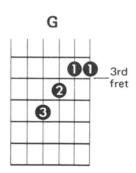

Again the 4th finger of the left hand plays the hammer-on and snap-off grace notes:

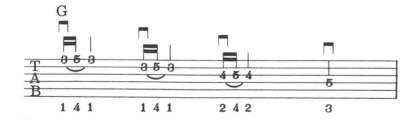

Practice the bounce on some of the other *root 6 bar chords* you know. It is a very pretty figure and quite popular with soul and R & B lead guitarists.

The next and last solo illustrates how the many scales you know fit together when improvising. The chord background of the progression is the popular *turn-around* progression and is the last cut on side two of the record. Listen to it a few times.

Now play the progression with the record. The E minor chord is fingered at the 12th fret.

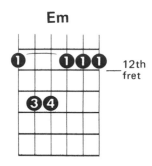

TURN AROUND IN G #1

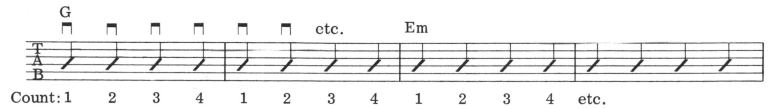

In the progression each chord lasts for two measures. During these two measures a single scale or technique is used to improvise with. The scale used is notated so as to give you a better idea of how to use these new scales. Practice the solo for awhile until it presents no problems—then try it with the record.

TURN AROUND IN G #2

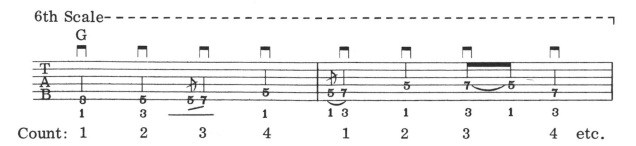

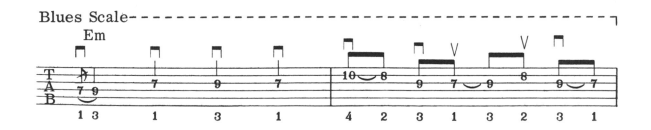

104

Bounce

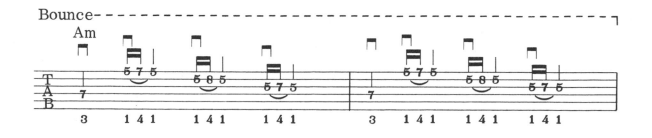

6th Scale

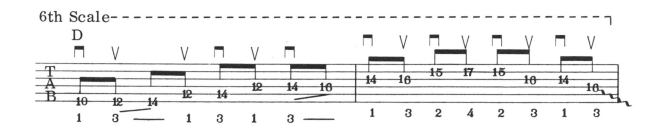

Bounce

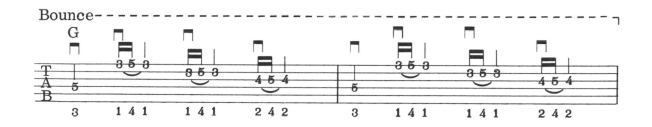

Minor Jazz Scale

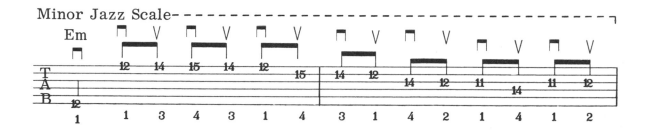

Blues Scale

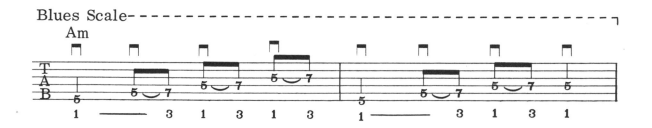

Country Blues Riff

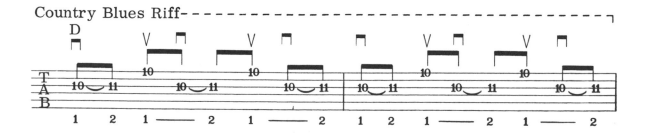

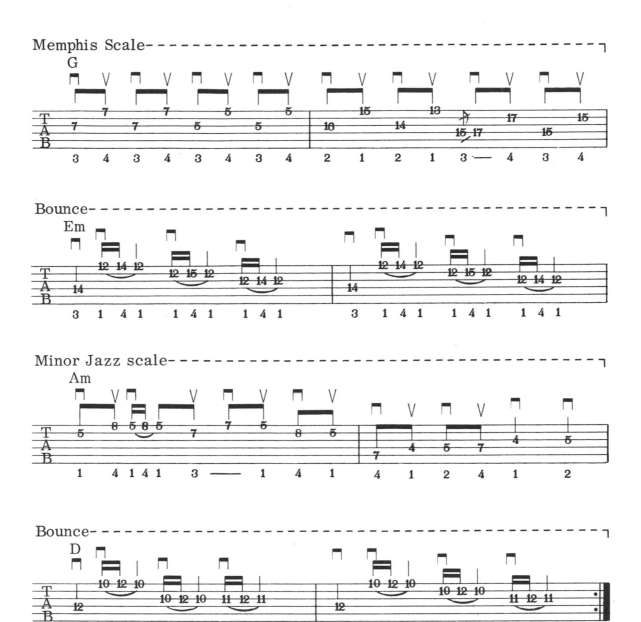

Try creating some of your own solos and play them with the turn-around progression on the record. Use the scales presented in this lesson and any of the other riffs and techniques you've learned. Play the turn-around progression in other keys such as A: A /A /F#m/F#m/Bm /Bm /E /E // Improvise to this progression using the same techniques as with the turn-around in G. This will give you experience in improvising with other minor chords.

In Conclusion

There are countless other riffs and ideas and concepts that you need to pick up on and I could show them to you but this book would become too complicated, sophisticated, regulated, and over-ornamented. So you're going to have to do some hustling on your own: like buying records, playing stoned, rapping with other guitarists, and trying to bite into something substantial that you can communicate to your fingers.

How about taking some lessons? A word to the wise—stay away from middle-aged, middle-class, establishment music teachers unless that's your trip. Take lessons from a rock lead guitarist. Preferably someone who plays in a band. Preferably someone who reads and understands what he's playing.

Remember, learning to play good lead is like learning how to talk. At first all you do is crap around with the pick and try to keep the strings in tune and worry about holding the guitar correctly and worry about playing too loud or not playing loud enough and about the way you look and is your hair long enough or too long? After you've made that trip, you'll start thinking about the music and what you're playing and how you're playing it and whether it sounds right when you play it. In other words, you'll start listening to the sounds you're creating. And then one day you'll see those six shiny strings waiting to be caressed and told what to do and you'll feel it—the blues I mean. You'll flip on your amp, turn up your guitar and begin to say and play what you always wanted to. And you'll feel the juice flowing out of your four 12" Lansing speakers and it'll feel good and you'll know it's there because that's what keeps you going. And you'll wonder who in the hell ever said New York is an island? And that's what the rock revolution is all about and that's what blues is all about and that's what lead guitar is all about.

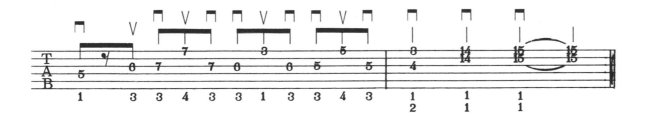

... music is your special friend,
Dance on fire as it intends,
Music is your only friend
Until the end, until the end. *
—The Doors

Appendix A

RECORDS AND STUFF TO KNOW . . .

Here's a list of rock groups and records that you should be familiar with. They provide an excellent foundation for any rock musician's record library. These are the best records of every style on the rock scene—the best of the best. Like everything involved in pop culture, styles change and new groups come on the scene so you'll have to augment this selection from time to time.

When listening to these records, there are some definite questions that you can ask that are necessary to a well-rounded evaluation. These questions were compiled by Jerry Coker in his excellent book *Improvising Jazz.* *

1. *Choice of Materials.* Does the artist make use of the best songs available? Is the song appropriate for the player's style and interpretation?

2. *Emotional Content.* Does his tone quality seem alive? Is he able to project, emotionally?

3. *Versatility.* How many different moods is he able to create? Does he adapt to new musical environments and establish rapport with others in the group? Is the excitement he creates limited to swing, rhythmic outbursts, humor, and mischief? Or does the excitement also take on the more subtle aspects of beauty, thoughtfulness, sincerity, sweetness, and melancholy?

4. *Taste.* Is the chosen mood always appropriate to the musical situation? Does he practice moderation and economy in using his materials and techniques?

5. *Originality.* Is the artist an innovator? Though he might show that he has absorbed the qualities of other players, is there a considerable amount of material which seems to be his own, so that one is actually able to distinguish him from other artists of a similar style? Does there seem to be a creative urge about him which causes his style to be constantly enriched with new ideas?

6. *Intellectual Energy.* Can the player hold one's interest with only the stimulus of his ingenuity? Is the player physical, cerebral, or both?

You might also ask these questions of your own playing and your group's.

*IMPROVISING JAZZ
by Jerry Coker
© Copyright 1964
Reprinted by permission of Prentice-Hall, Inc.
Englewood Cliffs, New Jersey

RHYTHM 'N BLUES

History of Rhythm & Blues (Atlantic 8161, 8162, 8163, 8164)
Chicago / The Blues / Today! (Vanguard 9216)
The Blues (Cadet 4026, 4027, 4034)
Elmo James, *The Sky is Crying* (Sphere 7002)
Slim Harpo, *Raining in My Heart* (Excello 8003)
Jimmy Reed, *The Best of Jimmy Reed* (Vee Jay SR 1039)
Chuck Berry, *Chuck Berry's Greatest Hits* (Chess 1483)
Jr. Walker and the All Stars, *Shotgun* (Soul 701)
T. Bone Walker, *The Truth* (Brunswick BL 754126)

MODERN AMERICAN

Jimi Hendrix, *Jimi Hendrix Experience Smash Hits* (Reprise 2025)
Country Joe & The Fish, *Electric Music for the Mind and Body* (Vanguard 79244)
The Doors, *The Doors,* (Elektra 74007)
The Young Rascals, *The Young Rascals* (Atlantic 8123)
Big Brother and the Holding Company, *Cheap Thrills* (Columbia KCS9700)

FOLK ROCK

Jefferson Airplane, *Surrealistic Pillow* (RCA 3766)
Crosby, Stills & Nash, *Crosby, Stills & Nash* (Atlantic SD 8229)
The Band, *Music From Big Pink* (Capitol SKAO 2955)
Moby Grape, *Moby Grape* (Columbia CS 9498)
Bob Dylan, *Bob Dylan's Greatest Hits* (Columbia KCS 9463)
Donovan, *Sunshine Superman* (Epic LN 24217)

THE DETROIT SOUL SOUND

The Mar-keys & Booker T. & the MG's, *Back to Back* (Stax 720)
Otis Redding, *The Otis Redding Dictionary of Soul Complete & Unbelievable* (Volt 415)
Otis Redding, *Otis Blue* (Volt 412)
Wilson Pickett, *The Best of Wilson Pickett* (Atlantic 8151)
Sam & Dave, *The Best of Sam & Dave* (Atlantic SD-8218)
James Brown, *James Brown at the Garden* (King 1018)
Sly & the Family Stone, *Stand!* (Atlantic SD-8229)

BLUES BANDS

B. B. King, *Live at the Regal* (ABC-Paramount 509)
Blues Breakers, *Blues Breakers* (London 492)
Charley Musselwhite's Southside Band, *Stand Back!* (Vanguard 79232)
The Paul Butterfield Blues Band, *What's Shakin'* (Elektra 4002)
Johnny Winter, *Johnny Winter* (Columbia CS 9826)
Taj Mahal, *The Natch'l Blues* (Columbia CS 9698)
Albert King, *Live Wire / Blues Power* (Stax 2003)

MODERN ENGLISH

Cream, *Best of Cream* (Atco SD33-291)
Jethro Tull, *Stand Up* (Reprise 6360)
The Beatles, *Sgt. Pepper's Lonely Hearts Club Band* (Capitol 2653)
        Abbey Road (Apple SO-383)
The Rolling Stones, *Big Hits (High Tide and Green Grass)* (London NP-1)
Ten Years After, *Ssssh. Ten Years After* (London DES 18029)
The Who, *Tommy* (Decca DXSW 7205)
Led Zeppelin, *Led Zeppelin* (Atlantic SD 8216)

Appendix B

SUGGESTIONS FOR BUYING A GUITAR

There are two types of rock 'n roll guitars: the solid body and the semi-hollow body.

The solid body guitar has a very "funky" sound, and is preferred by blues bands and hard-rock groups. It produces very intense high notes, and the metallic, wailing quality makes it an excellent lead guitar as well as a hard and gutty rhythm guitar.

The semi-hollow body has some of the qualities of an acoustic guitar, and has a softer, mellower tone. This characteristic makes a better instrument for the jazz or folk influenced rock styles prevalent among many of today's bands. It should be remembered that it is the guitarist that controls the sound, and, with some experimentation with your guitar and amplifier, you should be able to get any sound you want out of your instrument.

Some professionals like to use a regular round-hole acoustic guitar with a built-in pick-up for certain sounds and effects. The quality of the tone here is very close to that of the unamplified guitar but, of course, much louder. Many country-western and "rock-a-billy" groups have pick-ups installed in their Martins and Gibsons, and bridge the gap between country and rock music. This is also used by several prominent folk rock artists where the sound is consistent with the music and their particular style. It is, however, very limiting for the all-around rock 'n roll guitarist.

Before you decide which to buy, try out several different makes and types of guitars at a music store. The kind of guitar you get will greatly affect the sound of your music, so the decision is an important one.

Once you have decided on the type of guitar you want, there is still the problem of getting the best guitar for your money. If you have never bought a guitar before, I would strongly urge you to take a guitar-playing friend or teacher to the store with you. Here are several important things to look for before buying a guitar:

Is the neck perfectly straight? Sight along the fingerboard from the nut as if you were aiming a rifle. You will be able to see if the neck is bent or twisted in any way. A warped neck will usually mean that the frets are not in correct tune, which will be a problem later on. For good luck, turn the guitar around and check it again from the bridge to the nut.

Most of the better guitars have an adjustable rod built into the neck to prevent warping.

Are the frets in tune? Pluck each string open, and then fretted at the 12th fret. The notes should be perfect octaves. If the two notes don't sound in tune, the frets might not be placed properly, or the neck might be warped. If the guitar has a movable bridge, it might only need readjusting. But these are questions for a person experienced in these matters.

Is the action too high or too low? Many electric guitars have devices that allow you to adjust the action (distance of the strings from the fingerboard). If the action is too high, it will be difficult to fret the strings properly, especially with bar chords. If it is too low, your strings will buzz (hit the frets while vibrating) and the tone will be poor. If the action is not comfortable one way or the other, see if the bridge can be adjusted to make the strings higher or lower. On some guitars there will be a screw at the place where the neck joins the body, which changes the angle of the neck, thereby changing the action. If these features are not built into the guitar and the action is not right, a qualified repair man would be needed to change it. It would probably be better to buy a different guitar.

Other things to check: Are the frets smooth and of even height? Do the volume and tone controls work easily and noiselessly? How about the tuning pegs—are they easy to turn, and do they tune the strings evenly and accurately?

These things are all important; much more important than the size, shape, color and designs and fancy decorations that adorn some electric guitars.

AMPLIFIERS

You also need an amplifier. There are many inexpensive amps you can get to practice with, and if you're really strung out for bread you can even play your guitar through a radio or T.V. (The sound's not fantastic, but at least you can hear yourself play.) When you are ready to join a group, you'll have to buy a better amp. It's important that you have one that does not distort or blow out at high volumes and that has reverb. If you can afford one that has vibrato and super-treble, so much the better.

Do yourself a favor: when you are ready to play in a group, buy yourself the best equipment you can afford. Cheap guitars and amps will cost you more money in the long run than you saved by buying them. I recommend Fender and Les Paul for solid body guitars, Gibson or Guild for semi-hollow body guitars. If you are buying an acoustic, Martins and Gibsons are my choice.

The best amps are made by Fender, Standell, and Ampeg.

ACCESSORIES

Many contemporary lead guitarists use special equipment to add interest to their playing. Equipment such as fuzz tones (cause the sound to distort), wah-wah pedals (simulate a muted trumpet), tone generators (simulate an organ), treble boosters (bring out the highs), volume boosters (increase the output of the amp), volume pedals, tone-control pedals, echo machines, etc. Experiment with devices of this type to see if one or more of them fit the kind of sound you want to produce.

White collared conservatives flashing down the street,
Pointing their plastic fingers at me.
They're hoping soon my kind will drop and die,
But I'm gonna wave my freak flag high,
Wave on, wave on.
                                        —Jimi Hendrix